ॐ = mc²

Spirituality and Science

CW00486326

Navaratri
Science and The Bhakti of Shakti

Author: Rajesh Joshi
Copyrights © Rajesh Joshi, 2020
First Edition July 2020

Preface

While the rest of the world is trying to find happiness using materialistic means and looking outward, Hinduism from the east believes happiness is an inner experience and provides means to achieve with self-exploration or looking inward. Yoga and Meditation techniques are an example of this which are helping millions of people to overcome, stress, anxiety, depression, and other mind-related diseases.

Hinduism is a science-based religion. All rituals and traditions of Ancient India have deep science behind. The tradition of Navaratri also has science and spiritual background.
In this book, I have attempted to explore the science and spirituality of Navaratri. I have also provided a complete guide on how to worship the Divine Mother, Goddess Shakti. This book is a presentation style format to provide simple and to the point explanation.

This work is dedicated to the following:
Thousands of Rishis, Yogis, and Sadhus of Indian origin
My parents Smt. Shanti Joshi and Tikam Chandra Joshi
My wife, Reeta Joshi

Contents

Hinduism is based on Science

Hindu spirituality encourages questioning everything

Hinduism is a Science-based religion

Most of the Hindu scriptures are a dialogue between two or more sages. The incredible thing about Hindu Spirituality is that questions are encouraged.

Hindu scriptures like Bhagawat Gita, Mahabharata, Ramayana, Vijnana Bhairava, and thousands more are based on questions and answers.

"In Hinduism, most of the scriptures were written because, someone asked a question"

Status of Science in Ancient India

Science and Mathematics were highly developed during the ancient period in India. Most Indian scriptures Vedas, Sutras, Purana, Mahabharata, Ramayana, and thousands more contain science.

Hinduism is based on Science

It is incredible to know that many theories of modern-day mathematics and science were known to ancient Indians. However, since ancient Indian scientists followed oral tradition, the majority of knowledge was spread through speech and was not documented.

Over time the majority of knowledge acquired by ancient Indians has been lost. However, in the past hundreds of years, the world has rediscovered this ancient knowledge and has documented and claimed as their own.

Moreover, the invaders ruled over most of the world for a long time. This empowered invaders to claim superiority in every way, including in the field of knowledge.

Here are the important discoveries of ancient India.

❖ Discovery of Pi, Zero and Infinity
❖ Decimal & Binary number system, Ruler, Weighing scale
❖ Discovery of Algebra, Calculus, Trigonometry, calculation of area of circle and sphere, length of an arc, chord, Permutation and Combination, and First Order equation
❖ Bodhayana Theorem now known as Pythagoras theorem
❖ Discovery of the equator line, the discovery of various planets, earth's orbit and Surya Siddhanta
❖ The shape of the earth, the discovery of Gravity by Brhamagupta, Quantum Mechanics, Astrophysics and Astrology
❖ Discovery of Yoga and Meditation
❖ Discovery of Ploughing, Cotton and Jute Cultivation
❖ Sugar refinement, Metallurgy, Zinc, Steel and Lead refinement
❖ The first school of medicine, Ayurveda and Siddha medicine, cataract surgery, first nasal surgery, plastic surgery and anaesthesia
❖ The first book of grammar by Panini
❖ Game of Chess, Kabaddi, and Ludo
❖ The first education system called Gurukul

Hinduism is based on Science

The primary objective of the development of the science during ancient India was the need to have accurate calendars, predict rainfall patterns, develop a better understanding of climate change timely sowing and choice of crops, navigation, fixing the dates of seasons and festivals, casting of horoscopes for use in astrology, calculation of time

During ancient times, for trade reasons, crossing the oceans and deserts during the night hours required a robust navigation system. The knowledge of astronomy was used to predict the tides, movement, and location of stars.

Like many rituals in Hinduism, Navaratri also has excellent science behind which is explained in this book.

$$\cdots + n^2 = {n(n + 1)(2n + 1) \over 6}$$

$$+ 2^3 + \cdots + n^2 = (1 + 2 + \cdots + n)^2$$

Dating Birth of Scientists and Hindu Scriptures

It is not easy to date the exact time of the birth of these scientists especially when other civilizations are continuously claiming superiority. Thousands of Indian youth are now researching and reviving Indian history in its originality. It is impressive to find that how recent evidence-based research is dating Indian history much older than what the vested interest group dated it in the past.

India's Scientific Tradition

**Modern Science is only 400 years old.
India has over 10000 years of scientific heritage.**

Over 10,000 years
Indian Scientific Tradition

400 years
Modern Science

Kapila Muni · Kanada Rishi · Gautama · Patanjali · Charak · Aryabhatta · 140,000 Texts · 1000's of Scientist

Galileo · Kepler · Newton · Einstein · Neil Bohr, Planck · Schrodinger · Heisenberg

**Indian Science
Last 10,000 Years
Since 8000 BC and more**

**Modern Science
Last 400 Years
1600 CE till now**

Outsiders Approach to India's Scientific Heritage

Ignorance and misinterpretation: There is no relation between Science and Spirituality AND there is no scientific History of India

eYogi's & 21st Century Views

Acceptance of Profound Vedic and Yogic Science:
Mind, Matter, Science and Spirituality are connected

The Bhakti of Shakti

In the Shakta philosophy, Shiva is never changing, eternal, pure consciousness. Shakti is his energy or kinetic power. The universe is a manifestation of this energy. Shiva is the omnipresent and inactive element, the pure consciousness. Meanwhile, Shakti is dynamic.
The creation is not possible without both. Hence, they are one.

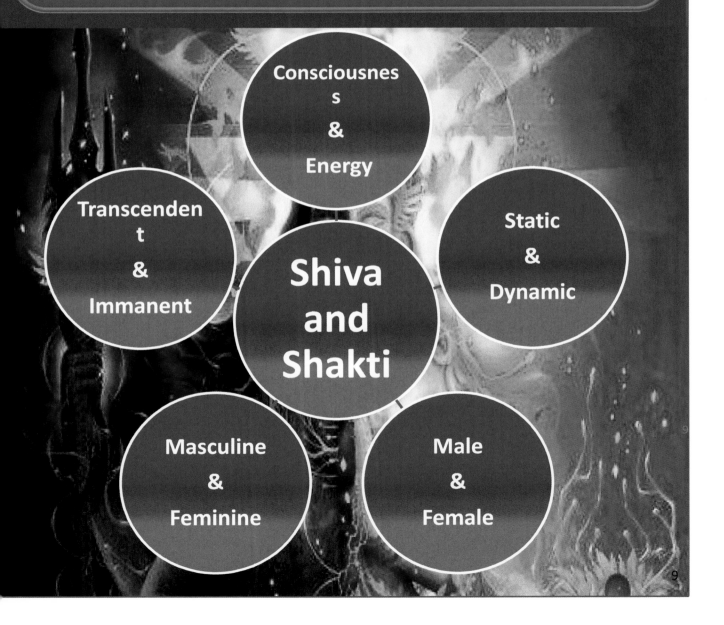

Nature and its Transitions

To understand the science behind the Navaratri, let us first understand the transitions of nature.

There are four apparent transitions in nature.

1. **Trikala**
   - ❖ 3 Times during the day - Sandhyas

2. **Lunar Phases – Purnima and Amavasya**
   - ❖ 2 Phases of the moon

3. **Paths of the Sun**
   - ❖ 2 Paths – Northern and Southern Hemisphere

4. **Seasonal Shifts**
   - ❖ 4 Seasons
     - ➢ Winter
     - ➢ Spring
     - ➢ Summer
     - ➢ Autumn

Trikala
3 Times of the Day (Sandhya)

There are three critical times in a day.

1. Brahma Sandhya (Morning)
2. Vishnu Sandhya (Noon)
3. Mahesh Sandhya (Evening)

Lunar (Moon) Phases

- The Hindu calendar is based on Lunar Phase
- Most festivals are celebrated based on various phases of the moon
- Purnima is called "Full Moon" and Amavasya is called "Dark Moon"
- Waxing Phase is from Amavasya to Purnima
- Waning Phase is Purnima to Amavasya

Tithi (Date)	Divas (Day)	Paksha (Hindu Lunar Phase)	Lunar Phase	Tithi (Date)	Divas (Day)	Paksha (Hindu Lunar Phase)	Lunar Phase
	Amavasya	Krishna	Dark Moon		Purnima	Shukla	Full Moon
1	Pratipada	Shukla	Waxing	1	Pratipada	Krishna	Waning
2	Dwitiya	Shukla	Waxing	2	Dwitiya	Krishna	Waning
3	Tritiya	Shukla	Waxing	3	Tritiya	Krishna	Waning
4	Chaturthi	Shukla	Waxing	4	Chaturthi	Krishna	Waning
5	Panchami	Shukla	Waxing	5	Panchami	Krishna	Waning
6	Shashthi	Shukla	Waxing	6	Shashthi	Krishna	Waning
7	Saptami	Shukla	Waxing	7	Saptami	Krishna	Waning
8	Ashtami	Shukla	Waxing	8	Ashtami	Krishna	Waning
9	Navami	Shukla	Waxing	9	Navami	Krishna	Waning
10	Dasami	Shukla	Waxing	10	Dasami	Krishna	Waning
11	Ekadasi	Shukla	Waxing	11	Ekadasi	Krishna	Waning
12	Dvadasi	Shukla	Waxing	12	Dvadasi	Krishna	Waning
13	Trayodasi	Shukla	Waxing	13	Trayodasi	Krishna	Waning
14	Chaturdashi	Shukla	Waxing	14	Chaturdashi	Krishna	Waning
	Purnima	Shukla	Full Moon		Amavasya	Krishna	Dark Moon

Paths of the Sun
Uttarayan and Dakshinayana

- The earth rotates on its axis of 23.5 degrees. This tilted rotation causes the hemispheric difference, which leads to different seasons like winter and summer.
  - Hemi = Half, Sphere = Ball
- There are two Hemispheres

- **Uttarayana (Northern Hemisphere)**
  - Summer months: May, June, July (June 21 to Sep 21)
  - Sunrise: Northeast, peaks out slightly south of the overhead point
  - Sunset: in the Northwest

- **Dakshinayana (Southern Hemisphere)**
  - Summer months: November, December, January (Sep 21 to Jun 21)
  - Sunrises: Southeast, peaks out slightly north of the overhead point
  - Sunset: in the Southwest

Uttarayana and Dakshinayana

Uttarayana
Northern Hemisphere

Dakshinayana
Southern Hemisphere

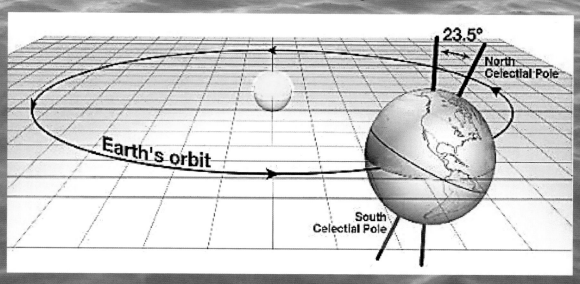

Uttarayana Festivals

- The first day of the sun's transit into Makara (Capricorn) has a special significance in Science and Hinduism. It marks the end of the month with the winter solstice and the start of longer days.

- Uttaryana starts on the 14th or 15th of January every year. India celebrates the following festivals;
    - *Makar Sankranti* commonly known
    - *Magh Bihu* in Assam
    - *Maghi* (preceded by *Lohri*) in Punjab
    - *Pongal* in Tamil Nadu
    - *Ghughuti* in Uttarakhand
    - *Pedda Pandaga* in Andhra Pradesh and Telangana, *Poush Sankranti* in West Bengal
    - *Khichadi* in Uttar Pradesh
    - *Kumbh Mela* begins on this day

The 4 Navaratris

Navratri	Northern Hemisphere	Southern Hemisphere	Navaratri Hindu Calendar Month	Navratri English Calendar Month
Maagh Navarati	Winter	Summer	Maagh	January – February
Vasant Navaratri	Spring	Autumn	Chaitra	March – April
Ashad Navaratri	Summer	Winter	Ashad	June – July
Sharad Navaratri (Maha Navarati)	Autumn	Spring	Ashwin	September - October

"Nav" means 9, "Ra" = that gives solace, "Tri" = 3 types of Solace

"Ratri" is what gives you solace from 3 types of sufferings

| Physical pain | Mental sufferings | Causal past Karmas |

Navaratri or 9 nights are the nights where one seeks solace from all sufferings and gets rejuvenated

The 9 nights resemble the 9 months of a mother's pregnancy, and a child is born. After 9 nights of solace, one makes a fresh start in life.

What is Navaratri ?

Navaratri
The method to build strong Immune System

Science

- When the weather changes, flu seasons usually occur. We experience two primary shifts in the weather each year.

1. From *winter to summer*
   - Mostly occur during the months of Spring (Mach-April)

2. From *summer to winter*
   - Mostly occur during the months of Autumn (Sep-Oct)

Navaratri

Two Navaratris take place during these weather changes.

1. **Chaitra or Vasant Navratri** is observed

2. **Sharad or Maha Navratri** is observed

18

Navaratri
The method to build strong Immune System

Science

- Diet change: Not all crops grow all year round. When the seasons change, different crops are harvested. This results in a change in our diet.

- Detoxifies the body for 7 to 10 days

- Hygiene – Maintain a high level of hygiene

Navaratri

- Simple, less spicy, and vegetarian foods are eaten during Navaratri to prepare for a change in diet pattern.

- More water, juices, and other liquids are consumed which help in detoxification of the body from previous weather season

- Before prayers, one takes a bath. One to two times prayers means 1-2 bath/day morning and evening. To offer Bhog (first offering of food to the deity), one has to prepare it first by taking a bath, cleaning the house, kitchen, and all utensils. No one is allowed to touch the food until the offering is complete. So, very high standards of hygiene are practiced during Navaratri.

Navaratri
The method to build strong Immune System

Science

Navaratri helps to develop Self-Discipline, a strict routine, and develop good habits to align with new weather patterns. It takes 7 to 10 days of strict discipline to build a healthy habit.

Navaratri also helps in developing robust mental health.

Navaratri

Vrat and Fasting
- Vrat (Vow of Devotion) is practiced with a Fast. Vrat, means one accepts the rules of restrictive discipline along with Upavasa or Fasting.
- Modern science has finally caught up with the benefits of fasting. Intermittent Fasting (IF) has beneficial effects on weight, body composition, cardiovascular biomarkers, and aging. It is a viable weight-loss method if maintained for a long time.
- By waking up early, one aligns with the sunrise time. After ten days of repetition, it becomes a habit.

Mental Strength Development
During Navaratri, mental strength is developed by invoking the power within. Mantras and auspicious environment lifts the mood and positivity flows

Science Behind Navaratri

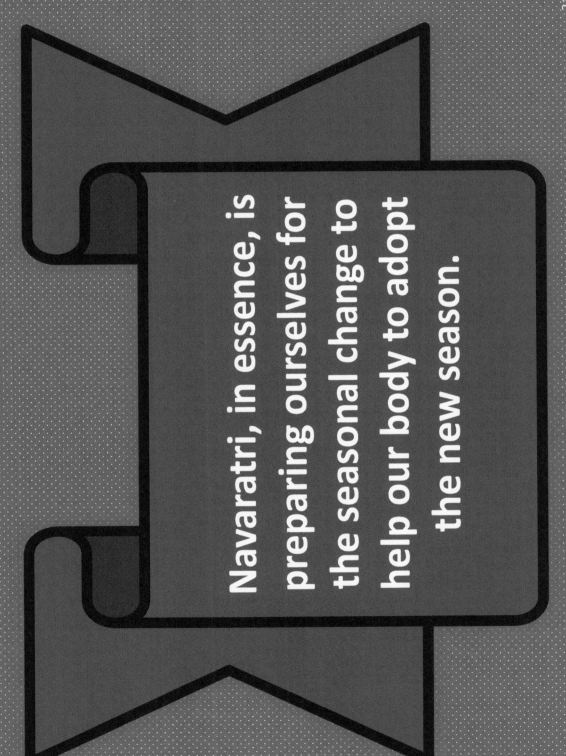

Navaratri, in essence, is preparing ourselves for the seasonal change to help our body to adopt the new season.

History of Navaratri

- It is not easy to date the origin of Navaratri celebration.

- Navaratri is the tale of Durga, a fierce form of the Divine Mother, who rides a lion and conquers the evil Mahisasura.

- In Hinduism, the concept of a divine feminine aspect of God can be traced back as far as any written texts, and human memory exists. The first text of humanity and Hinduism, called Vedas, contains several aspects of the divine forces of the universe.

- Ramayana contains prayers of divine mother and Shakti. The tenth day of Sharad Navaratri is known as Vijayadashami or Dussehra, where Rama defeated and killed the evil king Ravana.

- Mahabharat contains prayers of divine mother and Shakti

- Several Puranic texts have full details about mother Goddess and praying for Shakti

- Markandeya Purana, from Chapter 81 to Chapter 93, is the most influential text of Shaktism. The 700 slokas (verse) of 13 chapters are called Durga Saptashati, Chandi Path, and Devi Mahatyamam.

- The Purana have their origin in oral traditions where stories have been told generations after generations, so the roots of Durga Saptasasati goes back to thousands of years.

Shaktism

Shaktism is comprehensive and it has various Devis, texts, shrines, and temples associated with it.

- ➢ **9 Durga (Nav Durga)**
- ➢ **10 Mahavidyaye**
- ➢ **16 Matrikaya**
- ➢ **18 Maha Shakti Peeth**
- ➢ **51 Shakti Peeth**
- ➢ **64 Yoginis**
- ➢ **108 names of Durga**
- ➢ **1000 names of Devi Lalita**
- ➢ **Ghandharvis, Devis, Apsaras and Yakshanis**
- ➢ **Puran - various Puran Texts**
- ➢ **Tantra Texts**

Agamas

The Agamas are theological treatises and practical manuals of divine worship. They include tantras, mantras, and yantras.

The Agamas are divided into three sections

1

2

3

The Shaiva for the followers of Shaivism

The Vaishnava for the followers of Vaishnavism

Shakta for the followers of Shaktism

Shakta Agamas

These are the glories of Shakti as the Mother Goddess. These dwell on the Shakti (energy) aspect of God and prescribe the worship of the Divine Mother in various forms using various ritualistic practices. Similar to Puran in nature, there are 77 Shakta Agamas. Shakta Agama texts are usually in the form of dialogues between Shiva and Parvati. In these texts, Parvati is asking questions to Shiva, and He is answering to Parvati.

Nav Durga

Here are the 9 forms of Devi.

1. Shailaputri
2. Brahmacharini
3. Chandraghanta
4. Kushmanda
5. Skandamata
6. Katyayani
7. Kalaratri
8. Mahagauri
9. Siddhidhatri

9 Days Significance

Days	Symbolism	Devi	Reciting
Day 1 Day 2 Day 3	Energy Power	Maha Kali	Durga Kavacham
Day 4 Day 5 Day 6	Wealth	Maha Lakshmi	Argala Stotram
Day 7 Day 8 Day 9	Knowledge	Saraswati	Keelak Stotam

Nav Durga
The 9 Forms of Energies

1. **Shailaputri** – Shail means that which rises like a mountain. She represents the peak of the energy that a living can ever experience.

2. **Brahmacharini** – Represents the ultimate infinite energy present in the universe. It invokes the same energy within us where one develops the mastery of mind and senses where one can abstain from food and water for a long time. It tells us how to dedicate ourselves when we want to attain something despite all challenges.

3. **Chandraghanta** – Chandra means moon, and ghanta is bell shape. Wherever we see the energy that forms the beauty of the universe, it is because of the mother Divine.

Nav Durga
The 9 Forms of Energies

4. **Kushmanda** – This is the form of energy that created the universe. Kushmanda is the Adi Shakti or first energy. It is believed that she has created this energy with a smile.

5. **Skandamata** – This is the motherly form of energy which takes care of this universe.

6. **Katyayani** – It is the form of energy forms the lives and destroys the negative energy and darkness.

7. **Kalaratri** – This is the dark energy that bonds this entire universe. Despite being dark, it brings solace and comfort and lives to this universe.

Nav Durga
The 9 Forms of Energies

8. **Mahaguari** – This is the most beautiful form of the energy which liberates us from all bondages

9. **Siddhidatri** – This form of energy which fulfills the desires which make things possible. Siddhidatri is the energy that is turned into some useful purpose

Spiritual Significance of Navaratri

As per Puran text, the Devi (Mother Deity of Power) defeated various demons during these 9 nights. In spiritual significance these demons are the bad qualities within.

Asura (Demon)	Spiritual Significance
Madhu and Kaitabha	Craving and Aversion
Mahishasura	Laziness and Dullness
Mund	Without body. Only talking no actions. The bad quality of a person when one just keeps talking but not actions.
Chund	Without a head or brain. Actions without knowledge. The bad quality of a person when one performs actions without any thought.
Shumbh	Doubting yourself
Nishumbh	Doubting others
Raktbeej	The wrong genes, past Karmas. Why one should perform good Karmas
Dhumra Lochana	The unclear vision

Nav Durga

Stories of Each Devi
Shailaputri, Brhmacharini and Chandraghanta

Day 1
Shailaputri

On the first day of Navaratri, people worship a form of Shakti called Shailaputri. Goddess Shakti represents a pure, divine female power. In Sanskrit, 'Shail' means mountain, and 'Putri' means daughter. Together they mean "daughter of the mountain." This is the legend of Shailaputri.

Day 2
Brahmacharini

On the second day of Navratri, people worship Maa Brahmacharini. In Sanskrit, 'Brahma' means penance, and 'Charini' means a female follower. During her childhood, Sage Narada reminded Parvati of her past life as Sati. He told her that there was still a chance for her to marry Shiva if she carried out penances. Parvati practiced a very strict Tapa, which pleased Shiva, and they got engaged.

Day 3
Chandraghanta

On the third day of Navratri, we worship a form of Goddess Shakti called Ma Chandraghanta. Parvati did not want her family or Shiva to feel embarrassed. Parvati transformed herself into a petrifying form called Chandraghanta. In this form, Parvati prayed to Shiva and begged him to change his form into a more lavish one. She asked him to dress up his marriage procession as well.

Stories of Each Devi
Kushmanda, Skandamata and Katyayani

Day 4
Kushmanda

On the fourth day of Navratri, we worship the form of Goddess Shakti, Ma Kushmanda. In Sanskrit, 'Ku' means little, 'Usha' means energy, and 'Anda' means egg. Together it means 'little cosmic eggs.' The story of Ma Kushmanda goes back to way before the universe even existed. From Her smile, a 'little cosmic egg' was produced. The 'little cosmic egg' refers to divine energy. This energy created the universe.

Day 5
Skandamata

Goddess Parvati had another son called Kartikeya. Kartikeya killed two asuras Tarakasura and Surapadman, along with all the demons that followed, and brought peace to the Gods. He had another name called Skand. Therefore, Parvati was given the name 'Skandamata,' meaning the 'mother of Skand.'

Day 6
Katyayani

There was a sage named Katyayan, who was a dedicated follower of Goddess Shakti. His greatest wish was for her to be born as his daughter. He prayed endlessly for his wish to be granted. Meanwhile, a demon called Mahishasura, who was part Water Buffalo, was growing stronger day by day, which distressed the Gods. When Gods worshipped to Shakti, she came for rescue and born as the daughter of sage Katyayan and thus named Katyayani. She killed Mahishasura.

33

Stories of Each Devi
Kalaratri, Mahagauri and Siddhidhatri

Day 7
Kalaratri

On the seventh day of Navaratri, we worship the form of Goddess Shakti called Kalaratri, also known as Maa Kaali. Kalaratri is believed to destroy all demons, ghosts, and negative energies. She is also believed to be the destroyer of time and death. Although intimidating in appearance, this Devi is kind towards all worshipers.

Day 8
Mahagauri

On the eighth day of Navratri, we worship the form of Goddess Shakti called Mahagauri. Mahagauri translates to extremely white or fair. Due to extreme penance to Pavarti turned dark and dirty. When Shiva visited her and pleased with her penance, he cleaned Parvati in Ganga water, and she started glowing radiantly and called as Mahagauri

Day 9
Siddhidhatri

On the last day of Navaratri, we worship the form of Shakti called Siddhidatri. Siddhidatri translates to "the one who fulfills wishes." It is believed Siddhidatri has given 18 powers to Shiva and also turned His body as half women; thus, Shiva became Artdhnarishvar. Using that, Brahma was able to create living beings.

Das Mahavidya
10 Forms of Goddess Shakti

- Legend: When Parvati got married to Shiva, one day, she wanted to attend the Yajna (fire ritual) organized by her father despite not invitation. She took Shiva's dissent as if Shiva was treating her as an ignorant lady. So she assumed different forms to show Shiva who she is. Parvati's anger manifested into ten Mahavidya of ten directions. These ten forms of Goddess are known as the Das Mahavidyas. Each form has a name, its attributes, story, and mantras. People practice these mantras to gain wisdom and learn the inner truth.

- Das Mahavidya is a group of ten aspects of Adi Shakti of Hinduism.

- These are all forms of Goddess Shakti.

- "Das" means "Ten" "Maha" means "Great" and "Vidya" means "Knowledge"; therefore, "Das Mahavidya" is "Goddesses of great knowledge."

- Brihat Dharma Purana has full details of these Mahavidyas.

Das Mahavidya
10 Forms of Goddess Shakti

Kali	Tara	Shodashi	Bhuvaneshvari	Bhairavi

Chinnamasta	Dhumavati	Bagalamukhi	Matangi	Kamala

Das Mahavidya
10 Forms of Goddess Shakti

1. • Kali (काली) - For the removing malefic effects of Saturn. Protection from evil forces.

2. • Tara (तारा) - Compassionate Goddess. For the immense abundance in all sphere of life.

3. • Shodashi (षोडशी) - The Goddess who is 16 Years Old. For power and happiness. For the removal of worries, fears, and evil spirits.

4. • Bhuvaneshvari (भुवनेश्वरी) - The creator of the world. For fame, and success.

5. • Bhairavi Maa (भैरवी) - Removal of doubts, malefic energies, and anxieties. Gives power and radiance.

6. • Chinnamasta (छिन्नमस्ता) - The self-decapitated Goddess. For the removal of dark forces, speedy success, and removal of obstacles.

7. • Dhumawati (धूमवती) - The Goddess who widows herself. For the spiritual upliftment and all-round success.

8. • Bagalamukhi (बगलामुखी) - The Goddess who seizes the tongue. For the victory, and protection.

9. • Matangi (मातंगी) - For the knowledge, wisdom, and mystical powers.

10. • Kamala (कमला) – For the health, protection and support of life.

Shodash Matrika

- Shodash means 16 and Matrika means mothers. Hence, Shodash Matrika means 16 Mother Goddesses.

- In some traditions across India, the 16 forms of mother Goddess is worshipped. During various poojas and rituals, 16 names of mother Goddess is invoked.

- All the 16 incarnations of Durga are collectively worshiped in almost all Hindu poojas and named Shodash Matrika Sangh

Shodash Matrikas

Gauri, Padma, Sachi, Medha, Savitri, Vijaya, Jaya, Devsena, Swadha, Swaha, Matarah, Lokamatrarh, Dhriti, Pushti, Tushti and Atman Kuldevi

ॐ गोर्यै नमः ॐ पद्मायै नमः। ॐ शच्यै मः। ॐ मेधायै नमः ॐ सावित्र्यै नमः। ॐ विजयायै नमः। ॐ जयायै नमः। ॐ देवसेनायै नमः। ॐ स्वधायै नमः। ॐ स्वाहायै नमः। ॐ मातृभ्यो नमः। ॐ लोक मातृभ्यो नमः ॐ धृत्यै नमः ॐ पुष्ट्यै नमः ॐ तुष्ट्यै नमः ॐ आत्मनः कुलदेवतायै नमः

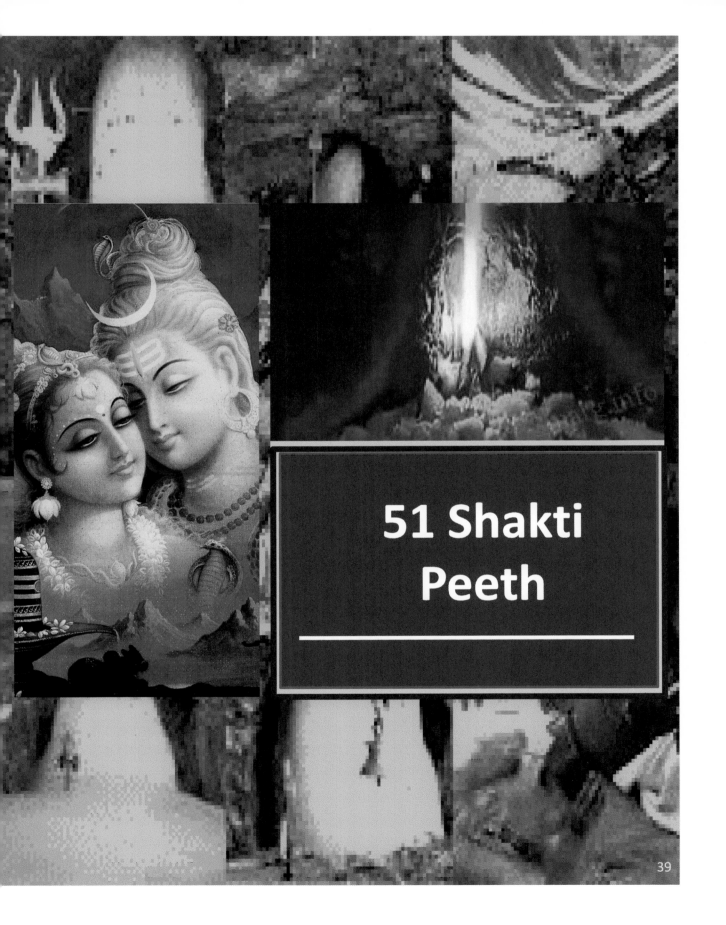

51 Shakti Peeth

Story of 51 Shakti Peeth

As per the ancient Hindu scriptures, the son of Brahma, King Prajapati Daksha, had a daughter named Sati. During Sati's childhood, Sage Narada and Brahma came to visit her in the palace. They reminded Sati of why she came to this world and her mission to marry Shiva. Years later, Sati decided to carry out a penance. Sati was extremely dedicated. Gods and Sages came to watch her. They were blown away by her extreme focus and passion. Shiva also observed Sati, and he, too, was appalled by her devotion. He appeared before Sati and extended her one boon. Sati asked for them to get married. Shiva granted the boon, and the pair got happily married in Daksha's palace.

A few years later, Brahma planned a grand yagna with lots of guests, including Shiva and Sati. When Daksha arrived at the event, every soul bowed down to him. The only people who did not bow down to Daksha were Brahma and Shiva. This incident provoked Daksha. In a fit of rage, Daksha cursed Shiva. Nandi became enraged and began to retaliate, then Shiva intervened and assured everyone that he had not been cursed. Everyone began to leave. Daksha returned home with a newfound grudge.

Story of 51 Shakti Peeth

A while later, Sati noticed that people were traveling to an event. After inquiring, Sati realized that there was a yagna taking place and being hosted by none other than her father, Daksha. Sati rushed home and told Shiva about her father's yagna and how they were not invited. Sati was furious, but she also missed her family very much. She decided that she will go to the yagna.

However, her father continuously ignored her presence. This kind of behavior or her father annoyed Sati, and she began preaching how no yagna could be complete without Shiva. Daksha proceeded to insult Sati and Shiva. Hearing Daksha insult her family was unbearable for Sati. She was horrified that Daksha also broke their agreement. Sati became so humiliated that she threw herself into the sacrificial fire.

Shiva's Ganas narrated the painful death of Sati to him. From his hair, Shiva created two forms, Virabhadra and Bhadrakali, and ordered them to destroy the yagna. Virabhadra got carried away and decapitated Daksha and killed others. After the horrific event, Shiva resuscitated those who died and gave them blessings. Shiva revived Daksha replacing the decapitated head with the sacrificed sheep's head. Daksha apologized to Shiva and spent the rest of his years as a devotee of Shiva.

Story of 51 Shakti Peeth

Grief-stricken, Shiva started the destruction of the universe while carrying Sati's body around the universe, recollecting their memories. Lord Vishnu realized that Shiva is going to destroy the universe. To pull Shiva out of grief, Vishnu intervened. Lord Vishnu cut Sati's body into 51 parts, which fell on the earth. The spots where the parts landed became holy sites, and people started to pray to mother Goddess. These 51 sites are called Shakti Peethas.

All of these Shakti Peeth also contains the shrine of Lord Bhairava. Bhairava is the manifestation of Lord Shiva. Lord Bhairava is the consort of the Goddess Shakti and accompanied her in all these Shakti Peeth.

It is challenging to produce an accurate list of the 51 Shakti Peethas. The ancient names of the places mentioned in the scriptures are not very specific in the modern context. There seems to be more than one name for the same place. As a result, more than 51 places have been identified as Shakti Peeth today. However, there is a specific list of 18 Maha Peethas from Skanda Puran and hymns composed by Adi Guru Shankaracharya.

18 Maha Shakti Peetha
by Adi Guru Shankaracharya

Number	Peetha Place	Body Part	Shakti Name
1	Trincomalee (Sri lanka)	Groin	Shankari devi
2	Kanchi (Tamil nadu)	Naval	Kamakshi Devi
3	Praddyumnam (West Bengal)	Stomach part	Sri Srunkhala devi
4	Mysore (Karnataka)	Hair	Chamundeshwari devi
5	Alampur (Andhra Pradesh)	Upper teeth	Jogulamba devi
6	Srisailam (Andhra Pradesh)	Neck part	Bhramaramba devi
7	Kolhapur (Maharastra)	Eyes	Mahalakshmi devi
8	Nanded (Maharastra)	Right hand	Eka Veerika devi
9	Ujjain (Madhya Pradesh)	Upper lip	Mahakali devi
10	Pithapuram (Andhra Pradesh)	Left hand	Puruhutika devi
11	Jajpur (Odisha)	Navel	Biraja devi
12	Draksharamam (Andhra Pradesh)	Left cheek	Manikyamba devi
13	Guwahati (Assam)	Vulva	Kamarupa devi
14	Prayaga (Uttar Pradesh)	Fingers	Madhaveswari devi
15	Jwala (Himachal Pradesh)	Head part	Vaishnavi devi
16	Gaya (Bihar)	Breast part	Sarvamangala devi
17	Varanasi (Uttar Pradesh)	Wrist	Vishalakshi devi
18	Srinagar (Kashmir)	Right hand	Saraswathi devi

18 Maha Shakti Peetha
by Adi Guru Shankaracharya

लङ्कायाम् शांकरीदेवी कामाक्षी काञ्चिकापुरे।
प्रद्युम्ने शृङ्खला देवी चामुण्डा क्रौञ्चपट्टणे॥
अलम्पुरे जोगुलाम्ब श्रीशैले भ्रमराम्बिक।
कोल्हापुरमहॅलक्ष्मी माहर्यमेकवीरिका॥
उज्जयिन्याम् महाकाळी पीठिकायाम् पुरुहतिका।
ओड्ढ्यायाम् गिरिजादेवी माणिक्या दक्षवॉटिके॥
हरिक्षेत्रे कामरूपी प्रयागे माधवेश्वरी।
ज्वालायाम् वैष्णवीदेवी गयामाङ्गल्यगौरिके॥
वारणास्याम् विशालाक्षी काश्मीरेतु सरस्वती।
अष्ठादशैवपीठानि योनिनामप दुर्लभानिच॥
सायंकालं पठेन्नित्यम् सर्वरोगनिवारणम्।
सर्वपापहरम् दिव्यम् सर्वसम्पत्करम् शुभम्॥

Lankayam Shankari devi, Kamakshi Kanchika pure
Pradyumne Shrinkhala devi, Chamunda Krouncha pattane
Alambapure Jogulamba, Sri shaile Bhramarambika
Kolha pure Maha lakshmi, Mahurye Ekaveerika
Ujjainyam Maha kali, Peethikayam Puruhutika
Odhyane Girija devi, Manikya Daksha vatike
Hari kshetre Kama rupi, Prayage Madhaveshwari
Jwalayam Vishnavi devi, Gaya Mangalya gourika
Varanasyam Vishalakshi, Kashmire tu Saraswati
Ashtadasha Shakti peethani, Yoginamapi durlabham
Sayamkale pathennityam, Sarva shatri vinashanam
Sarva roga haram divyam, Sarva sampatkaram shubham

- Goddess Shankari in Sri Lanka, Kamakshi in Kanchipuram Goddess Shrinkhala in Pradymna and Chamunda in Mysore
- Goddess Jogulamba in Alampur, Goddess Brhamarambika in Sri Shailam Goddess Maha Lakshmi in Kolhapur and Goddess Eka Veera in Mahur
- Goddess Maha Kali in Ujjain, Purhuthika in Peethika Goddess Girija in Odhyana and Manikya in the house of Daksha
- Goddess Kama Rupi in the temple of Vishnu, Madhaveshwari in Prayagraj Goddess giving flame in Jwala Mukhi and Mangala Gowri in Gaya
- Goddess Vishalakshi in Varanasi, Saraswati in Kashmir These are the 18 houses of Shakthi, which are rare even to the Devas
- When chanted every evening, all the enemies would get destroyed, all the diseases would vanish, and prosperity would be showered.

44

64 Yogini

It is believed that eight great female Shakti emerged from the Universal Shakti called "Para Shakti." These are called Ashta Matrika or Divine Grand Mothers of all subsequent Yoginis. These 8 Matrikas manifested each in turn into eight sacred Shakti, thus resulting in the 64 Tantric Yoginis.

The Divine Mother Shakti is also known as the great ascetic or Maha Yogini.

There are several references to 64 Yoginis in various Hindu scriptures like Agni Purana, Skanda Purana, Chandi Purana of Sarala Das, and many more.

The Lalitha Sahasranama and Vishnu Bhagavatha Purana reverently refer to Yogini.

The Yoginis are not only worshipped in Hinduism but also in Buddhism and Jainism.

Lalita Sahasranama
Thousand names of the Hindu mother Goddess Lalita

Lalita Sahasranama ललिता सहस्रनाम is an ancient text from Brahmanda Purana.

The text is simply a thousand names of the Hindu Mother Goddess, Lalita.

Goddess Lalita Devi is the divine manifestation of Shakti, the Mother Goddess. This text is the sacred text of Shakta tradition and worships Durga, Parvati, Kali, Lakshmi, Saraswati, Bhagavati, and many more.

Devi Shakti Lalita is described as being present in the form of Kundalini energy in the Muladhara chakra, which is at the bottom of the spine. The 60 names from 475 to 534 are the 60 Yoginis that are present from Muladhara to Sahasrara Chakra.

This text is used in various modes for the worship of the Shakti. This includes parayana (recitations), archana, and homa.

How to Worship Shakti

Can Women be Priests in Hinduism

To understand this, we need to go back to history during the Vedic Period 3000 years and before.

During the Vedic Period, women had all access to education. More importantly, several of them became seers of a very high order, displaying an intellectual and spiritual depth that is second to none. They are called Brahmavadinis, the speaker and revealers of Brahman - the infinite source of spirituality and pure consciousness.

Maa Sharada

Women were fully entitled to Upanaya and Brahmacharya, initiation, and Vedic studentship equally with men. They used to perform Poojas, Yajnas at home, and were also priests.

The Rig Veda contains hymns composed by as many as 27 **Brahmavadinis** or women seers like **Gosha, Godha, Vishwavara, Apala, Lopāmudrā, Maitreyi** and many more.

Respect of Women in Hindu Society

Women were respected and valued in Vedic society. On the one hand, women were regarded as mothers for bringing in a new generation, on the other hand, they were the individuals with great potential to perceive the truth and contribute richly to human society. Vedas and Upanishads encourage women to become a priest and seers.

Amma

India experienced Islamic invasion for 800 years and the British invasion for 150 years. Especially during the Islamic invasion, women were not safe; when captured, they were raped and sold as sex slaves to Arab and their army. To protect their women from invaders, the family used to hide girls and women, restrict their movement and started a veil tradition. This veil tradition resulted in limiting women's rights and freedom.

Mira Bai

Since 1947, post-Independence, the condition of women has significantly improved. More and more women are joining the spiritual community and also becoming priests.

Women Seers of Vedic Period

Maitreyi

The Rig Veda contains about ten thousand six hundred hymns. Maitreyi, a woman seer and Philosopher, has written about 10 hymns in Rig Veda. She also helped her sage-husband Yajnavalkya's and enhanced his spiritual thoughts.

Gargi

Gargi was an intellect being and possessed an excellent understanding in the issues related to creation. There were many texts authored by her in respect to Brahma Jnana. Gargi was the daughter of sage Vachaknu. Gargi composed several hymns that are related to the origin of all existence. She was one of the Navaratnas (9 Jewels) in the court of King Janaka.

Women Seers of Vedic Period

Gosha

Ghosha, was the daughter of Kakshivat and the granddaughter of Dirghatama. Gosha composed hymns in praise of Ashwins. In the 10th Mandala of the Rig Veda, Ghosha has two entire hymns of in containing each containing 14 verses, assigned to her.

Lopamudra

Lopamudra is another great sage of Vedic period. She is also known as Kaushitaki and Varaprada. Lopamudra was married to great Rishi Agastya. She was a female philosopher who has contributed towards Veda. Rig Veda contains long conversation between Lopamudra and her sage husband Agastya.

How often are Hindus supposed to pray

As per the Mimansa school of Vedas, Karmas are broadly classified into five types as follows:

1) Nitya Karma (Daily Karma)

❖ Daily obligatory towards Vedas, God, Gurus, Acharyas, and our ancestors. Veda mandates these Karmas and non-performance of these leads to sin Performing daily pooja morning and evening at your home

❖ Respecting your elders, parents, and teachers

2) Naimittika Karma (Occasional on specific events)

❖ Karmas which are performed occasionally based on certain calendar events and events in one's life

❖ Visit Local temple on special events like Holi, Diwali and Krishna birthday

❖ Doing special pooja at your home on particular dates of Hindu Calendar

My Karma (Duties)

1. **Perform Daily pooja morning and evening at your home**

2. **Perform Special Pooja on special events at your home**

3. **Attend special Pooja events at your local temple**

4. **Visit places of Hindu Pilgrimage every year**

How often are Hindus supposed to pray

3) Kamya Karma

- ❖ Rites to attain desired results. A set of activities carried out to achieve the various ends like Artha (Wealth) and Kama (Pleasure) while keeping up with the codes of conduct laid by Dharma
- ❖ Pilgrimage: Visiting Char Dham, Holy places, temples, and many more.

4) Prayaschitta Karma

- ❖ Karmas prescribed to compensate the sins and reduce the harmful impact of the past sins committed

5) Nishiddha Karma

- ❖ Forbidden action like unjustified killing. Performing these Karmas invoke sin

Sarva Mangala – Devi Sloka

This is the most common sloka recited by the worshipper for Devi.

Sarva-Mangala-Maangalye	सर्वमङ्गलमाङ्गल्ये
Shive Sarvartha-Saadhike ।	शिवे सर्वार्थसाधिके ।
Sharannye Tryambake Gauri	शरण्ये त्र्यम्बके गौरि
Naaraayanni Namostu Te ॥	नारायणि नमोऽस्तु ते ॥

1. (I worship to you O Narayani) Who is the auspiciousness in all the auspicious, auspiciousness Herself
2. Mother Goddess Shakti is complete with all the auspicious attributes, and Who fulfills all the objectives of the devotees (Purusharthas - Dharma, Artha, Kama, and Moksha),
3. Mother Goddess Shakti is the giver of refuge, with three eyes and a glorious face
4. Salutations to you, O Narayani!

Word by Word Meaning	
Sarva	= All
Mangala	= Auspicious
Mangalye	= Auspicious
Shive	= Consort of Lord Shiva
Artha	= Wealth
Sadhike	= Achiever
Sharanye	= Refuge of

Word by Word Meaning	
Trayambike	= The consort of the three-eyed person, Shiva
Gauri	= One with fair complexion (Parvati)
Narayani	= Parvati
Namah	= Salute
Astu	= Should happen
Te	= You

54

Books Related to Shakti

The original books that are related to mother Goddess Shakti are following:

- **Durga Kavach**
- **Argala Stotra**
- **Keelak Stotra**
- **Devi Sukta**
- **Devi Mahatmyam of Makendeya Puran**
- **Devi Bhagavata Purana**
- **Shiv Puran**
- **Soundarya Lahari of Adi Shankaracharya**
- **Lalitha Sahasranama**
- **Durga Chalisa**
- **Durga Aarti**

On the next page, we explain the difference between Mantra, Sloka, Stotra, and Stutis.

Sloka, Mantra Sukta & Stotra

- **Sloka**
  - Slokas are the melodious words from Chankkya Neeti, Meghdutam

- **Mantra**
  - Mantra is a phrase that has spiritual significance. These may not have any meaning. It can be a sound, a small text, or an extended composition, whereas slokas are verses only. The smallest mantra is OM, while there are very long mantras such as the Gayatri mantra and Mahamritunjaya mantra.

- **Sukta or Suktam**
  - Sukta is a Vedic hymn in praise of a God/Goddess.

- **Stotra, Stotram or Stutui**
  - These are groups of slokas put together to be melodically sung. It is always poetic in structure. Stotra is normally a prayer. Shatakam is a group of 6, ashtakam is a group of 8, and dashakam is a group of 10. Shiva Tandav Stotra,

9 Days Significance

On each day of Navaratri, people recite different Stotram and read Devi Mahatmyam book. Here is the list of these Stotram by each day.

Days	Reciting
1	Durga Kavacham Argala Stotram Keelak Stotam
2	Devi Mahatmyam Chapter 1 and 2
3	Devi Mahatmyam Chapter 3 and 4
4	Devi Mahatmyam Chapter 5 and 6
5	Devi Mahatmyam Chapter 7 and 8
6	Devi Mahatmyam Chapter 9 and 10
7	Devi Mahatmyam Chapter 11 and 12
8	Devi Mahatmyam Chapter 13
9	Devi Mahatmyam Durga Chalisa, Devi Suktam, Durga Aarti, Havan and Prasadam
10	Dashami Celebration

Devi Suktam
Auspicious Utterance to the Goddess

Origin

Devi Suktam is part of chapter 5 of "Devi Mahatmyam." Devi Mahatmyam is the 700 Slokas of the 13 chapters (81 to 93) of Markendeya Purana. These slokas are dedicated to Mother Goddess Durga and her glories, hence called "Devi Mahatmyam."

History

The two Asuras, Shumbh and Nishumbh became so powerful that they fought with all the Devatas and defeated them. They took over the offices of the Sun, the Moon, Kubera, Yama, Varuna, Vayu, and Agni.

Having deprived of their kingdom and expelled by these two great Asuras, all the

Devas thought of the invincible Devi, who is the symbolism of Shakti (power and energy). Devi is the form of Shakti known to help those who are in the worst calamities. Realizing this, Devas went to Himavat, lord of the mountains, and prayed to the Devi. They recited mantras in praise of Devi, and these are known Devi Suktam.

Devi Suktam - Slokas

Ya Devi Sarva-bhuteshu Viṣhṇu-mayeti Shabdita, Namas-tasyai, namas-tasyai Namas-tasyai, namo namaḥ.	To the Devi who in all beings, is called Shri Vishnumaya, Salutations to Her, Salutations to Her, Salutations to Her, again and again.
Ya Devi Sarva-bhuteshu Viṣhṇu-mayeti Shabdita, Chetanetya bhi-dhiyate, Namas-tasyai, namas-tasyai Namas-tasyai, namo namaḥ.	To the Devi who in all beings, is called Shri Vishnumaya, is termed as Consciousness, Salutations to Her, Salutations to Her, Salutations to Her, again and again.
Ya Devi Sarva-bhuteshu Buddhi rupena samsthita, Namas-tasyai, namas-tasyai Namas-tasyai, namo namaḥ.	To the Devi who in all beings, In the form of Intelligence, Salutations to Her, Salutations to Her, Salutations to Her, again and again.
Ya Devi Sarva-bhuteshu Nidra rupena samsthita, Namas-tasyai, namas-tasyai Namas-tasyai, namo namaḥ.	To the Devi who in all beings, In the form of Sleep, Salutations to Her, Salutations to Her, Salutations to Her, again and again.
Ya Devi Sarva-bhuteshu WORD samsthita, Namas-tasyai, namas-tasyai Namas-tasyai, namo namaḥ.	To the Devi who in all beings, In the form of Sleep, Salutations to Her, Salutations to Her, Salutations to Her, again and again.

Devi Suktam - Slokas

Now keep replacing the WORD from below and keep reciting the entire sloka

Word	Meaning
Kṣhudha rupena	Form of Hunger
Chhaya rupena	Form of Shadow
Shakti rupena	Form of Energy
Trishna rupena	Form of Thirst
Kṣhanti rupena	Form of Patience
Jati rupena	Form of Position by birth
Lajja rupena	Form of Modesty
Shanti rupena	Form of Peace

Word	Meaning
Shraddha rupena	Form of Faith
Kanti rupena	Form of Beauty
Lakṣhmi rupena	Form of Good Fortune
Vṛitti rupena	Form of Character
Smriti rupena	Form of Memory
Daya rupena	Form of Compassion
Tushti rupena	Form of Contentment
Matṛi rupena	Form of Mother
Bhranti rupena	Form of Delusion

श्री नवदुर्गा यन्त्रम्

सर्वमङ्गलमाङ्गल्ये शिवे सर्वार्थसाधिके ।
शरण्ये त्र्यम्बके गौरि नारायणि नमोऽस्तु ते ॥

Durga Kavach

Why Recite Devi Kavach?

- Durga Kavach is dedicated to Mahakali and its various forms
- There are 56 Slokas in this text

- Durga is the "Goddess of Shakti (power and energy)," and Kavach means "Armor." So this is the Armor of power and energy.

- Durga Kavach Summary
  - Sloka 1-2: Salutation to Mother Goddess Durga

  - Sloka 6-8: Why should one recite Durga Kavach?
    - Those who are frightened, having been surrounded by the enemies on the battlefield, or are burning in a fire, or being at an impassable place, would face no calamity, and would never have grief, sorrow, fear, or evil if they surrender to Durga.

  - Sloka 9-42: Describing the glories of all the forms of Devi Durga and praying for the protection of body, mind and all aspects of human life

  - Sloka 43-56: Benefits of reciting Devi Kavach

Why Recite Devi Kavach?

The positive psychology states that "We become what we repeatedly think." The ancient Rishis knew this secret, and that is why they recommended to remember the divine power and recite its glory, which gives strength. The Durga Kavach is a set of powerful mantras that acts as an armor for mental strength.

Those who having been surrounded by the enemies on the battlefield, are frightened or are burning in a fire, or being at an impassable place, would never have grief, and would face no calamity, fear, sorrow, or evil if they surrender to the Mother Goddess Shakti, the Durga.

जो मनुष्य अग्नि में जल रहा हो, रणभूमि में शत्रुओं से घिर गया हो, विषम संकट में फँस गया हो तथा इस प्रकार भय से आतुर होकर जो भगवती दुर्गा की शरण में प्राप्त हुए हों, उनका कभी कोई अमङ्गल नहीं होता।

युद्ध समय संकट में पड़ने पर भी उनके ऊपर कोई विपत्ति नहीं दिखाई देती। उनके शोक, दुःख और भय की प्राप्ति नहीं होती।

जिन्होंने भक्तिपूर्वक देवी का स्मरण किया है, उनका निश्चय ही अभ्युदय होता है। देवेश्वरि! जो तुम्हारा चिन्तन करते हैं, उनकी तुम निःसन्देह रक्षा करती हो।

अग्निना दह्यमानस्तु शत्रुमध्ये गतो रणे ।
विषमे दुर्गमे चैव भयार्त्ताः शरणं गताः ॥ ६॥

न तेषां जायते किंचिदशुभं रणसंकटे ।
नापदं तस्य पश्यामि शोकदुःखभयं न हि ॥ ७॥

यैस्तु भक्त्या स्मृता नूनं तेषां वृद्धिः प्रजायते ।
ये त्वां स्मरन्ति देवेशि रक्षसे तान्न संशयः ॥ ८॥

Agninaa Dahya_maanastu ; Shatrumadhye Gato Ra_Ne
Vishha_me Durgame chaiva , bhayaarh Sharanam Gataah |6|

Na Teshhaa.n Jaayate ; Kinchi_da_shubham_rana_sam_kaTe
Naapadam Tasya Pashyaami , Shoka_duhkha_bhayam na hi |7|

Yaistu Bhaktyaa Smritaa Nuunam ; Teshhaa.n vRiddhiH Prajaayate
Ye Tvaan Smaranti Deveshi ; Rakshase Taanna Sam_shayah |8|

॥ देवीकवचम् ॥

॥ Devi Kavacham ॥

(Sanskrit Stotra and Meaning)

From Devi Mahatmayam (This text is recited before the Devi Mahatmayam core text)

ॐ अस्य श्री चण्डीकवचस्य ॥

ब्रह्मा ऋषिः । अनुष्टुप् छन्दः । चामुण्डा देवता ।

अङ्गन्यासोक्तमातरो बीजम् । दिग्बन्ध देवतास्तत्त्वम् ।

श्रीजगदम्बाप्रीत्यर्थे सप्तशती पाठाङ्गत्वेन जपे विनियोगः ॥

Om Asya Sri Candi Kavachasya
Brahma Rishi | Anushtup Chandah |
Chaamunda Devata | Anganyasokta-Matari Bijam | Digbandha Devata-Astatvaṃ |
Sri-Jagadamba-Prityarthe Saptasati Pathangatvena Pape Viniyogah ||

Meaning

The Presiding Sage for Shri Devi-Kavach is Brahma Rishi; The Chanda (gauge) is Anushtup; The Presiding Deity is Chamunda Devi; The Beej Mantra is Anganyasakta Matar. The Principle Devata is Digbandha. This Stotram is recited as part of Durga Saptashati, to please Jagadamba Devi.

॥ ॐ नमश्चण्डिकायै ॥

Om Namashcandikyaih.

Meaning: Salutation to Candika Devi.

मार्कण्डेय उवाच ।

ॐ यद्गुह्यं परमं लोके सर्वरक्षाकरं नृणाम् ।

यन्न कस्यचिदाख्यातं तन्मे ब्रूहि पितामह ॥ १ ॥

Maarkandeya Uvaaca
Aum Yadh-goohyam Paramam Loke Sarva-Rakshakaram Nrinaman |
Yanna Kasya-Chidakhyatam Tanme Bruhi Pitamaha ||1||

Meaning 1:
Markandeya Rishi said:
O Brahmadeva, please tell me the ultimate secret which has yet not been revealed to anyone and which protects the human beings of this great world.

ब्रह्मोवाच ।

अस्ति गुह्यतमं विप्र सर्वभूतोपकारकम् ।

देव्यास्तु कवचं पुण्यं तच्छृणुष्व महामुने ॥ २ ॥

Brahmo uvaca|
Asti Goohya-Tamam Vipra Sarva-Bbhuto-Upakarakam |
Devya-Astu Kavacham Punyam Takshinashva Mahamune ||2||

Meaning 2:

Bramha said:

O Vipro (Brahmins), the most secret which is useful to all beings, is known as Devi Kavach. Please listen to this great Kavach where Devi Durga is known by the following names:

प्रथमं शैलपुत्री च द्वितीयं ब्रह्मचारिणी ।
तृतीयं चन्द्रघण्टेति कूष्माण्डेति चतुर्थकम् ॥ ३॥

Prathamam Shailaputri Dvitiyam Brahmacarini |
Trtiyam Candraghanteti Kushmanndeti Caturthakam ||3||

Meaning 3:

The first form of Durga is Shailputri; the second form is Brahmacharini, the third form is Chandraganta, and the fourth form is Kushmanda.

पञ्चमं स्कन्दमातेति षष्ठं कात्यायनीति च ।
सप्तमं कालरात्रीति महागौरीति चाष्टमम् ॥ ४॥

Pancamam Skandamateti Sastham Katyayaniti Ca |
Saptamam Kalaratri Mahagauriti Ca-Astamam ||4||

Meaning 4:

The fifth form of Durga is Skandamata, the sixth form is Katyayani, the seventh form is Kalaratri, and the eighth form is Mahagauri.

नवमं सिद्धिदात्री च नवदुर्गाः प्रकीर्तिताः ।
उक्तान्येतानि नामानि ब्रह्मणैव महात्मना ॥ ५॥

Navamam Siddhidatri Ca Nava-Durgah Prakirtitah |
Uktany-Etani Namani Brahmanaiva Mahatmana ||5||

Meaning 5:

The ninth form of Durga, Siddhidatri, grants Liberation. The great soul, Brahma, explained these names of Durga.

अग्निना दह्यमानस्तु शत्रुमध्ये गतो रणे ।
विषमे दुर्गमे चैव भयार्त्ताः शरणं गताः ॥ ६॥

Agnina Dahya-Manastu Shatrumadhye Gato Rane |
Vishame Durgame Chaiva Bhayarttah Sharanam Gatah ||6||

Meaning 6:
Those who are burning in a fire, having been surrounded by the enemies on the battlefield, facing difficult situations and frightened, should surrender to Durga.

न तेषां जायते किंचिदशुभं रणसंकटे ।
नापदं तस्य पश्यामि शोकदुःखभयं न हि ॥ ७॥
Na Teshhan Jayate Kinchida-Shubham Rana-Sankate |
Napadam Tasya Pashyami Shoka-Duhkha-Bhayam Na Hi ||7||

Meaning 7:
They would face no calamity on the battlefield; they would never have any sorrow, grief, and fear if they surrender to Devi Durga.

यैस्तु भक्त्या स्मृता नूनं तेषां वृद्धिः प्रजायते ।
ये त्वां स्मरन्ति देवेशि रक्षसे तान्न संशयः ॥ ८॥
Yaistu Bhaktya Smrita Nunam Teshan Vriddhiah Prajayate |
Ye Tvan Smaranti Deveshi Rakshase Taanna Samshayah ||8||

Meaning 8:
The one who remembers Devi Bhagavati with devotion, they find their paths, and Devi protects them without any doubt.

प्रेतसंस्था तु चामुण्डा वाराही महिषासना ।
ऐन्द्री गजसमारूढा वैष्णवी गरुडासना ॥ ९॥
Preta-Samstha Tu Camunda Varahi Mahishasana |
Aindri Gaja-Samaa-Rudha Vaishnavi Garudaasana ||9||

Meaning 9:
The Devi Camunda sits on a corpse, and the Devi Varahi rides on a buffalo; the Devi Aindri sits on an elephant and Vaishnavi on a Garunda (condor bird).

माहेश्वरी वृषारूढा कौमारी शिखिवाहना ।
लक्ष्मीः पद्मासना देवी पद्महस्ता हरिप्रिया ॥ १० ॥

Maheshvari Vrisha-Rudha Kaumari Shikhi-Vahana |
Lakshmih Padmasana Devi Padmahasta Hari Priya ||10||

Meaning 10:
The Devi Maheswari is riding on a bull, and the Devi Kaumari vehicle is a peacock, the Devi Lakshmi, who is very dear to Lord Vishnu, holding a lotus on Her hand also seated on a lotus.

श्वेतरूपधरा देवी ईश्वरी वृषवाहना ।
ब्राह्मी हंससमारूढा सर्वाभरणभूषिता ॥ ११ ॥

Shvetarupa-Dhara Devi Eishvari Vrishvahana |
Brahmi Hamsa-Samarudha Sarva-Bharana-Bhushita ||11||

Meaning 11:
The Devi Eishwari, riding on a bull, has white complexion. The Bhagavati Brahmani (Sarasvati) with all her ornaments seated on a swan.

इत्येता मातरः सर्वाः सर्वयोगसमन्विताः ।
नानाभरणशोभाढ्या नानारत्नोपशोभिताः ॥ १२ ॥

Ityeta Matarah Sarvah Sarvayoga-Samanvitah |
Nanaa-Bharana-Shobhadhyaa Nana-Ratnap-Shobhitah ||12||

Meaning 12:
All the forms of Devi are wearing various types of ornaments and appear graceful and attractive. All the forms of Devis are full of Yogic powers.

दृश्यन्ते रथमारूढा देव्यः क्रोधसमाकुलाः ।
शङ्खं चक्रं गदां शक्तिं हलं च मुसलायुधम् ॥ १३ ॥

Drishyante Rathamarudha Devyah Krodha-Sama-Kulah |
Shankham Cakram Gadam Shaktim Halam Ca Musala-Yudham ||13||

Meaning 13:

All the Devis are seated in chariots and appear very angry. The Devis are
All the Goddesses are seen mounted in chariots and very Angry. They are wielding
Shankha (Conch), Chakra (powerful discus), Gada(mace), Halam (ploughing tool), Musla
(javelin).

खेटकं तोमरं चैव परशुं पाशमेव च ।

कुन्तायुधं त्रिशूलं च शाङ्गमायुधमुत्तमम् ॥ १४॥

Khetakam Tomaram Caiva Parashum Pashameva Ca |
Kunta-Yudham Trishulam Ca Shangama- Aayudha-Muttamam ||14||

Meaning 14:

The Devis are wielding Khetak, Tomar, Parashu (Axe), Pash (tying rope), Trishul (Trident),
Shangmayudh (Bows and arrows).

दैत्यानां देहनाशाय भक्तानामभयाय च ।

धारयन्त्यायुधानीत्थं देवानां च हिताय वै ॥ १५॥

Daityaanam Dehanashaya Bhakta-Nama-Bhayaya Ca |
Dharayantya-Ayudha_Nitthan Devanam Ca Hitaya Vai ||15||

Meaning 15:

All these weapons wielded by various forms of Devis are to destroy the bodies of
demons, to protect the devotees and benefits of the Devas.

नमस्तेऽस्तु महारौद्रे महाघोरपराक्रमे ।

महाबले महोत्साहे महाभयविनाशिनि ॥ १६॥

Namaste-Astu Maha-Rudre Maha-Ghora-Parakrame |
Mahabale Mahotsahe Maha-Bhaya-Vinashini ||16||

Meaning 16:

Salutations to You, O Maharudre (the dreadful form of Devi), Mahaghorprakrame (the
ultimate frightening gallantry form of Devi), Mahabale (the tremendous powerful form
of Devi), Mahotsahe (the vibrant and energetic form of Devi), and the Mahabhaya-
Vinashini (the form that eradicates worst kind of fears).

त्राहि मां देवि दुष्प्रेक्ष्ये शत्रूणां भयवर्द्धिनि ।

प्राच्यां रक्षतु मामैन्द्री आग्नेय्यामग्निदेवता ॥ १७॥

Trahi Maam Devi Dush-Prekshye Shatrunam Bhaya-Vardhini |

Prachyam Rakshatu Maamaindri Aagney-Yam-Agni-Devata ||17||

Meaning 17:

O Devi, you create fear among your enemies, please protect me. May the Aindri Devi protect me from the east direction, and the fire Goddess Agni Devi protect me from the south-east Agnikon direction.

दक्षिणेऽवतु वाराही नैरृत्यां खड्गधारिणी ।

प्रतीच्यां वारुणी रक्षेद्वायव्यां मृगवाहिनी ॥ १८॥

Dakshine-Aavatu Varahi Nai-Rityam Khadga-Dharini |

Pratichyaan Varuni Raksheda-Vayavyan Mriga-Vaahini ||18||

Meaning 18:

May the Varahi Devi (the power of Lord Vishnu in the form of a wild boar) protect me from the south direction, the Khadgadharini Devi (wielder of the mighty sword) protect me from the south-west direction, the Varuni Devi (the power of rain God) protect me from the west direction, and the Mrgavahini (the Devi rides on a deer) protect me from the north-west direction.

उदीच्यां पातु कौमारी ऐशान्यां शूलधारिणी ।

ऊर्ध्वं ब्रह्माणि मे रक्षेदधस्ताद्वैष्णवी तथा ॥ १९॥

Udichyaan Patu Kaumari Aishanyaan Shuladharini |

Urdhvan Brahmani Me Rakshed-Dhastaad-Vaishnavi Tatha ||19||

Meaning 19:

May the Devi Kaumari (the power of Lord Kartikeya, son of Lord Shiva) defend me from the north direction, the Devi Shuldharini (Devi wielding trident) protect me from the north-east direction, the Devi Brahmani (the power of Lord Brahma) protect me from above, and the Devi Vaishnavi (power of Lord Vishnu) protect me from below.

एवं दश दिशो रक्षेच्चामुण्डा शववाहना ।

जया मे चाग्रतः पातु विजया पातु पृष्ठतः ॥ २०॥

Evam Dasha Disho Raksheca-Camunda Shava-Vahana |

Jaya Me Cagratah Paatu Vijaya Patu Prishthatah ||20||

Meaning 20:
May the Goddess who sits on a corps, the Camunda Devi, protect me from all ten directions.
May the Devi Jaya protect me from the front, and Devi Vijaya protect me from the rear.

अजिता वामपार्श्वे तु दक्षिणे चापराजिता ।
शिखामुद्द्योतिनी रक्षेदुमा मूर्ध्नि व्यवस्थिता ॥ २१॥

Ajita Vama-Parshve Tu Dakshine Ca-Parajita |
Shikham-Udayotini Rakshe-Duma Murdhini-Vyavasthita ||21||

Meaning 21:
May the Devi Ajita protect me from left and Aparajita from the right. May the Devi Dyotini protect me from the Shikha (top-knot), and Devi Uma sit on my forehead and Protect it.

मालाधरी ललाटे च भ्रुवौ रक्षेद्यशस्विनी ।
त्रिनेत्रा च भ्रुवोर्मध्ये यमघण्टा च नासिके ॥ २२॥

Maldhari Lalate Ca Bhruvau Rakshedh-Yashasvini |
Trinetra Ca Bhruvor-Madhye Yama-Ghanta Ca Nasike ||22||

Meaning 22:
May the Devi Maladhari (the one with a garland on her neck) protect me on the forehead, the Devi Yashsvini protect me on both eye-brows, the Devi Trinetra protect me between the eye-brows, the Devi Yamaghanta protect me on the nose.

शङ्खिनी चक्षुषोर्मध्ये श्रोत्रयोर्द्वारवासिनी ।
कपोलौ कालिका रक्षेत्कर्णमूले तु शाङ्करी ॥ २३॥

Shankhini Chakshu-Shormadhye Shrotrayor-Dwar-Vasini |
Kapolau Kaalika Rakshet-Karnamule Tu Shankari ||23||

Meaning 23:
May the Devi Shankhini protect me on both the eyes, the Devi Dwaravasini protect me on the ears, the Devi Kalika protect my lips, and the Devi Shankari protect the roots of the ears.

नासिकायां सुगन्धा च उत्तरोष्ठे च चर्चिका ।
अधरे चामृतकला जिह्वायां च सरस्वती ॥ २४॥

Nasikayam Sugandha Ca Uttaroshthe Ca Charchika |
Adhare Cham-Amrit-Kala Jihvayam Ca Sarasvati ||24||

Meaning 24:
May I be protected by Devi Sugandha on the nose, Devi Carchika on the lips, Devi Amrtakala on the lower lip, and Devi Saraswati on the tongue.

दन्तान् रक्षतु कौमरी कण्ठदेशे तु चण्डिका ।
घण्टिकां चित्रघण्टा च महामाया च तालुके ॥ २५॥

Dantaanh Rakshatu Kaumari Kanthadeshe Tu Candika |
Ghantika Citra-Ghanta Ca Mahamaya Ca Taluke ||25||

Meaning 25:
May I be protected by Devi Kaumari on the teeth, Devi Candika on the throat, Devi Citraghanta on the neck, and Devi Mahamaya on the upper jaw.

कामाक्षी चिबुकं रक्षेद्वाचं मे सर्वमङ्गला ।
ग्रीवायां भद्रकाली च पृष्ठवंशे धनुर्धरी ॥ २६॥

Kamakshi Chibukam Rakshedh-Vacham Me Sarvamangala |
Grivayam Bhadrakali Ca Prishtha-Vamshe Dhanurdhari ||26||

Meaning 26:
May I be protected by the Devi Kamakshi on the chin, Devi Sarvamangala my speech, Devi Bhadrakali on the neck, and Devi Dhanurdhari on the back.

नीलग्रीवा बहिःकण्ठे नलिकां नलकूबरी ।
स्कन्धयोः खड्गिनी रक्षेद्बाहू मे वज्रधारिणी ॥ २७॥

Nilagriva Bahihkanthe Nalikam Nalakubari |
Skandhayoh Khangini Rakshedh-Baahu Me Vajradharini ||27||

Meaning 27:
May I be protected by Devi Neelagreeva on the outer part of my throat, Devi Nalakubari on the windpipe, Devi Khadgini on the shoulders, and Devi Vajradharini on the arms.

हस्तयोर्दण्डिनी रक्षेदम्बिका चाङ्गुलीषु च ।

नखाञ्छूलेश्वरी रक्षेत्कुक्षौ रक्षेत्कुलेश्वरी ॥ २८ ॥

Hastayordandini Rakshedambika Cangulishu Ca |
Nakhanchuleshvari Rakshet-Kukshau Rakshet-Kuleshvari ||28||

Meaning 28:
May I be protected by the Devi on both hands, Devi Ambika on the fingers, Devi Shuleshwari on the nails, Devi Kuleshwari on the belly.

स्तनौ रक्षेन्महादेवी मनःशोकविनाशिनी ।

हृदये ललिता देवी उदरे शूलधारिणी ॥ २९ ॥

Stanau Rakshen-Mahadevi Manahshoka-Vinashini |
Hridaye Lalita Devi Udare ShuladhariNi ||29||

Meaning 29:
May I be protected by the Mahadevi on the breast, Devi Shokdharini on the mind, Devi Lalita on the heart, and Devi Shuldharini on the abdomen.

नाभौ च कामिनी रक्षेद्गुह्यं गुह्येश्वरी तथा ।

पूतना कामिका मेढ्रं गुदे महिषवाहिनी ॥ ३० ॥

Nabhau Ca Kamini Rakshedh-Guhyam Guhyeshvari Tatha |
Putana Kamika Medhram Gude Mahisha-Vahini ||30||

Meaning 30:
May I be protected by the Devi Kamini on the naval, Devi Guhyeshvari on the hidden parts, Devi Putana and Devi Kamana on the reproductive organs, and Mahishavahini on the excretory organ.

कट्यां भगवती रक्षेज्जानुनी विन्ध्यवासिनी ।

जङ्घे महाबला रक्षेत्सर्वकामप्रदायिनी ॥ ३१ ॥

Katiyan Bhagavati Rakshej-Januni Vindhya-Vasini |
Janghe Mahabala Rakshet-Sarvakama-Pradayini ||31||

Meaning 31:
May I be protected by the Devi Bhagavati on the waist, Devi Vindhyavasini on the knees, and Devi Mahabala, who fulfill all wishes, on the hips.

गुल्फयोर्नारसिंही च पादपृष्ठे तु तैजसी ।
पादाङ्गुलीषु श्री रक्षेत्पादाधस्तलवासिनी ॥ ३२॥

Gulphayo- Narasimhi Ca Pada-Pristhe Tu Taijasi |
Pada-Agulishu Shri Rakshet-Padadha-Stala-Vasini ||32||

Meaning 32:
May I be protected by the Devi Narashini on both ankles, Devi Taijasi on the backside of feet, Devi Shree on the toes, and Devi Talavasini on the soles of feet.

नखान् दंष्ट्राकराली च केशांश्चैवोर्ध्वकेशिनी ।
रोमकूपेषु कौबेरी त्वचं वागीश्वरी तथा ॥ ३३॥

Nakhanh Danshtra-Karali Ca Keshansh-Caivo-Urdhvakeshini |
Roma-Kupeshu Kauberi Tvacham Vagishvari Tatha ||33||

Meaning 33:
May I be protected by the Devi Danshtrakarali on the nails, Devi Urdhvakeshini on the hair, Devi Kauberi on the skin pores, and Devi Vagishwari on the skin.

रक्तमज्जावसामांसान्यस्थिमेदांसि पार्वती ।
अन्त्राणि कालरात्रिश्च पित्तं च मुकुटेश्वरी ॥ ३४॥

Raktamajjava-Sama-Saanya-Sthi-Medasi Parvati |
Antrani Kalaratrishca Pittam Ca Mukuteshvari ||34||

Meaning 34:
May I be protected by the Devi Parvati on the blood, bone marrow, fat, and bone. May I be protected by the Devi Kalaratri on the intestines, and Devi Mukuteshwari on the bile.

पद्मावती पद्मकोशे कफे चूडामणिस्तथा ।
ज्वालामुखी नखज्वालामभेद्या सर्वसन्धिषु ॥ ३५॥

Padmavati Padmakoshe Kaphe Cudamani_Stitha |
Jwalamukhi Nakha-Jvalam-Bhedya Sarva-Sandhishu ||35||

Meaning 35:
May I be protected by the Devi Padmavati on the chakras, Devi Choodamani on the lungs, Devi Jwalamukhi on the sheen of the nails, Devi Abhedya on all the joints.

शुक्रं ब्रह्माणि मे रक्षेच्छायां छत्रेश्वरी तथा ।
अहंकारं मनो बुद्धिं रक्षेन्मे धर्मधारिणी ॥ ३६॥

Shukram Brahmani Me Rakshe-Chaayam Chhatreshvari Tatha |
Ahamakaram Mano Buddhin Rakshen Me Dharma-Dharini ||36||

Meaning 36:
May I be protected by the Devi Brahmani on the semen, Devi Chhatreshvari on the shadow of the body, and Devi Dharmadharini on the Ahankar (ego or identity), Manas(mind), Buddhi (intellect).

प्राणापानौ तथा व्यानमुदानं च समानकम् ।
वज्रहस्ता च मे रक्षेत्प्राणं कल्याणशोभना ॥ ३७॥

Pranapanau Tatha Vyanamudanam Ca Samanakamh |
Vajrahasta Ca Me Raksheth-Pranam Kalyana-Shobhana ||37||

Meaning 37:
May the Vajrahasta Devi protect my 5 Prana Vayus (5 vital breathing forces) Pran, Apan, Vyan, Udan, and Saman. May the Devi bring auspiciousness, the Kalyanashobhana protect my Pranas (life force).

रसे रूपे च गन्धे च शब्दे स्पर्शे च योगिनी ।
सत्त्वं रजस्तमश्चैव रक्षेन्नारायणी सदा ॥ ३८॥

Rase Rupe Ca Gandhe Ca Shabde Sparshe Ca Yogini |
Sattvam Rajasta-Mash-Chaiva Rakshe-Narayani Sada ||38||

Meaning 38:
May the Devi Yogini protect the faculties of senses, tasting, seeing, smelling, hearing, and touching. May the Devi Narayni protect the three fundamental qualities of nature (guna), Satva, Rajas, and Tamas.

आयू रक्षतु वाराही धर्मं रक्षतु वैष्णवी ।
यशः कीर्तिं च लक्ष्मीं च धनं विद्यां च चक्रिणी ॥ ३९॥

Aayu Rakshatu Varahi Dharmam Rakshatu Vaishhnavi |
Yashah Kiirtim Ca Lakshmi Ca Dhanam Vidyam Ca Chakrini ||39||

Meaning 39:
May I be protected the Devi Varahi on the longevity, Devi Vaishnavi on the righteousness (Dharma), Devi Lakshmi on the fame and success, and the Devi Chakrini on the wealth, and knowledge.

गोत्रमिन्द्राणि मे रक्षेत्पशून्मे रक्ष चण्डिके ।
पुत्रान् रक्षेन्महालक्ष्मीर्भार्यां रक्षतु भैरवी ॥ ४० ॥
Gotramindrani Me Rakshet-Pashunme Raksha Chandike |
Putranh Raksh-Maha-Lakshmi-Bharyaan Rakshatu Bhairavi ||40||

Meaning 40:
May Devi Indrani protect my relatives, Devi Candika protect my cattle, Devi Mahalakshmi protect my children, and Devi Bhairavi protect my spouse.

पन्थानं सुपथा रक्षेन्मार्गं क्षेमकरी तथा ।
राजद्वारे महालक्ष्मीर्विजया सर्वतः स्थिता ॥ ४१ ॥
Panthanam Supatha Rakshen-Margam Kshemakari Tatha |
Rajadvare Maha-Lakshmi Vijaya Sarvatah Sthita ||41||

Meaning 41:
May Devi Supatha protect my travel, and Devi Kshemakari protect my path. Devi Mahalakshmi Protect me in the court, and Devi Vijaya protect me everywhere.

रक्षाहीनं तु यत्स्थानं वर्जितं कवचेन तु ।
तत्सर्वं रक्ष मे देवि जयन्ती पापनाशिनी ॥ ४२ ॥
Raksha-Hinam Tu Yatsthanam Varjitam Kavachena Tu |
Tatsarvam Raksha me Devi Jayanti Paapa-Nashini ||42||

Meaning 42:
O Devi Jayanti, protect me from all unprotected places that are not covered in this Devi Kavach.

पदमेकं न गच्छेत्तु यदीच्छेच्छुभमात्मनः ।
कवचेनावृतो नित्यं यत्र यत्रैव गच्छति ॥ ४३॥

Padamekam Na Gachhettu Yadichchhech-Chhu-Bhu-Aatmanah |
Kavachenavrito Nityam Yatra Yatraiva Gachchhati ||43||

Meaning 43:
If one seeks well being and protection, then one should not walk even a step without reciting the Devi Kavach.

तत्र तत्रार्थलाभश्च विजयः सार्वकामिकः ।
यं यं चिन्तयते कामं तं तं प्राप्नोति निश्चितम् ॥ ४४॥

Tatra Tatra-Arth-Labhashca Vijayah Sarva-Kamikah |
Yam Yam Cintayate Kamam Tam Tam Prapnoti Nishcitamh || 44 ||

Meaning 44:
The one who recites the Devi Kavach gains material wealth and enjoys success everywhere. One attains success, fame, and all desires are fulfilled.

परमैश्वर्यमतुलं प्राप्स्यते भूतले पुमान् ।
निर्भयो जायते मर्त्यः संग्रामेष्वपराजितः ॥४५॥

Paramaishvaram-Atulam Prapsyate Bhutale Pumaanh |
Nirbhayo Jayate Martyah Samgrameshva-Parajitah ||45||

Meaning 45:
Anyone who recites the Devi Kavach becomes fearless, is never defeated on the battlefield. One attains worthiness to be worshipped in all three lokas.

त्रैलोक्ये तु भवेत्पूज्यः कवचेनावृतः पुमान् ।
इदं तु देव्याः कवचं देवानामपि दुर्लभम् ॥ ४६॥

Trailokye Tu Bhavet-Pujyah Kavache-Navritah Pumanh |
Idam tu Devyah Kavacham Devanam-Api Durlabhamh ||46||

Meaning 46:
One who reads the Devi Kavach, which is not even accessible to Devas, with full devotion, is worshipped in the three lokas.

यः पठेत्प्रयतो नित्यं त्रिसन्ध्यं श्रद्धयान्वितः ।
दैवी कला भवेत्तस्य त्रैलोक्येष्वपराजितः ॥ ४७॥

Yah Patheth Prayato Nityam Trisandhyam Shraddhayan-Vitah |
Daivi Kala Bhavettasya Trailokyeshva-Parajitah ||47||

Meaning 47:
One who recites the Devi Kavach with full devotion during the three Sandhakala (morning, afternoon, and evening) attains Devikala (divine powers), is undefeated in the three worlds, lives for hundred years, and is undefeated.

जीवेद्वर्षशतं साग्रमपमृत्युविवर्जितः ।
नश्यन्ति व्याधयः सर्वे लूताविस्फोटकादयः ॥ ४८॥

Jiivedh Varsha-Shatam Sagrama-Pamrityur-Vivarjitah |
Nashyanti Vyadhayah Sarve Luta-Visphotaka-Udayah ||48||

Meaning 48:
One who recites the Devi Kavacha lives for a hundred years and free from premature death
All his diseases like scars, smallpox, and boils are eliminated.

स्थावरं जङ्गमं चैव कृत्रिमं चापि यद्विषम् ।
अभिचाराणि सर्वाणि मन्त्रयन्त्राणि भूतले ॥ ४९॥

Sthavaram Jangamam Caiva Kritrimam Chapi Yadvishmh |
Abhi-Carani Sarvani Mantra-Yantrani Bhutale ||49||

Meaning 49:
All the moveable poisons (from snakes, scorpions, ants, etc.) and immoveable poisons (created by humans) do not affect all the magical spells cast by mantras or yantras with band intention have not to affect those who recite the Devi Kavach.

भूचराः खेचराश्चैव जलजाश्चौपदेशिकाः ।
सहजा कुलजा माला डाकिनी शाकिनी तथा ॥ ५०॥

Bhucarah Khecharash-Caiva Jalajash-Choupa-Deshikah |
Sahaja Kulaja Mala Dakini Shakini Tatha ||50||

Meaning 50:
All the malevolent beings are moving on the earth, in the sky, and the water is destroyed.
The evil Gram Devatas originating with birth, the evil Kul Devata created in the Kula, the Dakinis (female goblins), Shakinis (another type of female goblins) are destroyed.

अन्तरिक्षचरा घोरा डाकिन्यश्च महाबलाः ।
ग्रहभूतपिशाचाश्च यक्षगन्धर्वराक्षसाः ॥ ५१ ॥

Antariksha-Cara Ghora Dakinyashchcha Mahabalah |
Graha-Bhuta-Pishachashchcha Yaksha-Ghandharva-Rakshasah ||51||

Meaning 51:
The mighty Dakinis wandering in the deep space are destroyed. The negative effect of planet positions, Bhoot, Pisach, Yaksha, Gandharva, and Rakshas, are destroyed.

ब्रह्मराक्षसवेतालाः कुष्माण्डा भैरवादयः ।
नश्यन्ति दर्शनात्तस्य कवचे हृदि संस्थिते ॥ ५२ ॥

Brahma-Rakshasa-Vetalah Kushmanda Bhairavadayah |
Nashyanti Darshanattasya Kavache Hridi Samsthite ||52||

Meaning 52:
All the Brahma Rakshas, Kushmand, and frightening Bhairavs are also destroyed.
All these evil entities are destroyed just by the sight of the person having Devi Kavach in his heart.

मानोन्नतिर्भवेद्राज्ञस्तेजोवृद्धिकरं परम् ।
यशसा वर्धते सोऽपि कीर्तिमण्डितभूतले ॥ ५३ ॥

Maano-Natir-Bhavedragyaste-Tejo-Vriddhikaram Paramh |
Yashasa Vardhate So-Api Kirti-Mandita-Bhutale ||53||

Meaning 53:
The person who recites Devi Durga Saptashati receives enormous respect from the King.
The fame and prosperity of the person rise on this earth.

जपेत्सप्तशतीं चण्डीं कृत्वा तु कवचं पुरा ।
यावद्धूमण्डलं धत्ते सशैलवनकाननम् ॥ ५४॥

Japet-Saptashati Candim Kritva Tu Kavacham Pura |
Yavad-Bhu-Mandalam Dhatte Sashaila-Vanakananamh ||54||

Meaning 54:
The one who recites the Durga Saptashati, his progeny (children and grandchildren), remains on this earth for the life the world contains forest, mountains, and wilderness.

तावत्तिष्ठति मेदिन्यां सन्ततिः पुत्रपौत्रिकी ।
देहान्ते परमं स्थानं यत्सुरैरपि दुर्लभम् ॥ ५५॥

Tava-Tishthati Medinyam Santatih Putra-Pautriki |
Dehante Paramam Sthanam Yatsurairapi Durlabhamh ||55||

Meaning 55:
Mother nature will be able to sustain the nourishment of progeny of one who recites the Durga Saptashati and attains the highest place that is inaccessible even to the Gods.

प्राप्नोति पुरुषो नित्यं महामाया प्रसादतः ।
लभते परमं रूपं शिवेन सह मोदते ॥ ॐ ॥ ५६॥

Prapnoti Purusho Nityam Mahamaya Prasadatah |
Labhate Paramam Ruupa Shivena Saha Modate || AUM |||56||

Meaning 56:
The one who recites the Durga Saptashati, by the grace of Devi Mahamaya, attains the highest place that is inaccessible even to the Devas and is eternally blissful in the company of Shiva.

॥ इति देवीकवचम् समाप्ति ॥
|| Durga Kavacham End ||

Argala Stotram

Argala Stotram

- Argala Stotram is dedicated to Maha Lakshmi and Her various forms.

- There are 25 Slokas in this text. There are two extra slokas added by some authors.

- Argala Stotram Sumary

  - Sloka 1-11 forms of the Durga and their names are described in this sloka.

  - Sloka 2-24: These slokas describe the various ways of praying Durga. These are all in praise of Durga Devi.

  - Sloka 3-23: These slokas contain the following words as the 2nd line. This is repeated in each sloka. Each sloka, when appropriately narrated, creates a beautiful musical rhythm.

रूपं देहि जयं देहि यशो देहि द्विषो जहि ॥
Ruupam Dehi Jayam Dehi Yasho Dehi Dvisso Jahi ||

O Devi, Please Grant me (Spiritual) Beauty, Please Grant me (Spiritual) Victory, Please Grant me (Spiritual) Glory and Please Destroy my (Inner) Enemies.
  - Sloka 25 : This sloka describes why one should recite Argala Stotram

---

Why Recite Argala Stotram?

The sloka invokes the 11 forms of Shakti which are associated with various auspicious qualities of human nature.

Jayanti (Who is always victorious), Mangala (Who provides Auspiciousness), Kali (Who is beyond time or Kala), Bhadrakali (Who is the controls the birth and death), Kapalini (Who wear a garland of skulls), Durga (Who removes obstacles), Shiva (Who is consort of Shiva the omni-present consciousness), Kshama (Who is an embodiment of forbearance), Dhatri (Who is the supporter of all beings), Swaha (Who is the final receiver of the Sacrificial oblations to Gods) and Swadha (Who is the final receiver of the Sacrificial oblations to manes).

इदं स्तोत्रं पठित्वा तु महास्तोत्र पठेन्नरः ।
सप्तशतीं समाराध्य वरमाप्नोति दुर्लभम् ।।

Idam Stotram Patthitvaa Tu Mahaastotra Patthen-Narah |
Saptashatiim Sama-[A]araadhya Varam-Aapnoti Durlabham | |

जो मनुष्य इस स्तोत्र का पाठ करके सप्तशती रूपी महास्तोत्र का पाठ करता है, वह सप्तशती की जप-संख्या से मिलने वाले श्रेष्ठ फल को प्राप्त होता है। साथ ही वह प्रचुर संपत्ति भी प्राप्त कर लेता है।।

After reading the Argala Stotra, one should then read the core text called Durga Saptashati. Argala Stotra is equally revered like the Saptashati; by reading this with devotion, one obtains difficult to receive boons.

॥ अर्गलास्तोत्रम् ॥

॥ Argala Stotram ॥

(Sanskrit Stotra and Meaning)

From Devi Mahatmayam (This is recited before the core text of Devi Mahatmayam)

जय त्वं देवि चामुण्डे जय भूतापहारिणि ।
जय सर्वगते देवि कालरात्रि नमोऽस्तु ते ॥१॥
Jaya Tvam Devi Chamunde Jaya Bhu Tapa Harini |
Jaya Sarvagate Devi Kalaratri Namostu Te ||1||

Meaning 1:

Victory to you, O Devi Chamunda, victory to you Devi, who is the remover of worldly distress and sorrows.

Victory to you, O Devi, you are present in all beings; Worship to you, O Devi Kalaratri.

जयन्ती मङ्गला काली भद्रकाली कपालिनी ।

दुर्गा शिवा क्षमा धात्री स्वाहा स्वधा नमोऽस्तु ते ॥२॥

Jayanti Mangala Kali Bhadrakali Kapalini |
Durga Shiva Kshama Dhatri Svaha Svadha Namostu Te ||2||

Meaning 2:

Salutations to Jayanti (the ever-victorious Devi), Mangala (the Devi bestows auspiciousness), Kali (the Devi who is beyond time or Kala), Bhadrakali (the Devi who controls the birth and death and beyond time or Kala), Kapalini (the Devi who wears a garland of skulls).

Salutations to the Durga (the Devi who eliminates bad happenings), Shiva (the Devi who is the consort of Lord Shiva), Kshama (the Devi who is an embodiment of forbearance), Dhatri (the Devi who supports all life and beings), Swaha (the Devi who is the final receiver of the sacrificial oblations to Devas) and Swadha (the Devi who is the final receiver of the sacrificial oblations to manes); Salutations to you, O Devi!

मधुकैटभविध्वंसि विधातृवरदे नमः ।

रूपं देहि जयं देहि यशो देहि द्विषो जहि ॥३॥

Madhu Kaitabha-Vidhvamsi Vidhatr-Varade Namah |
Rupam Dehi Jayam Dehi Yasho Dehi Dvisso Jahi ||3||

Meaning 3:

Salutations to Devi Durga, who destroyed the Madhu and Kaitabha, thus granting the boon of protection to Sri Brahma.

O, Devi! Please grant me beauty, victory, glory, and destroy my enemies.

महिषासुरनिर्नाशि भक्तानां सुखदे नमः ।

रूपं देहि जयं देहि यशो देहि द्विषो जहि ॥४॥

Mahisasura-Nirnashi Bhaktanam Sukhade Namah |
Rupam Dehi Jayam Dehi Yasho Dehi Dvisso Jahi ||4||

Meaning 4:
Salutations to Devi Durga, who destroyed the demon Mahishasura; Salutations to Devi, who gives ultimate joy her devotees.
O, Devi! Please grant me beauty, victory, glory, and destroy my enemies.

धूम्रनेत्रवधे देवि धर्मकामार्थदायिनि ।
रूपं देहि जयं देहि यशो देहि द्विषो जहि ॥५॥

Dhumranetra-Vadhe Devi Dharma-Kama-Artha-Dayini |
Rupam Dehi Jayam Dehi Yasho Dehi Dvisso Jahi ||5||

Meaning 5:
Salutations to Devi Durga who slew the demon Dhumralochana (Dhumranetra); Salutations to Durga, who gives the path of righteousness (Dharma), fulfills the worldly desires (Kama) and gives prosperity (Artha) to devotees.
O, Devi! Please grant me beauty, victory, glory, and destroy my enemies.

रक्तबीजवधे देवि चण्डमुण्डविनाशिनि ।
रूपं देहि जयं देहि यशो देहि द्विषो जहि ॥६॥

Raktabija-Vadhe Devi Chand-Mund-Vinashini |
Rupam Dehi Jayam Dehi Yasho Dehi Dvisso Jahi ||6||

Meaning 6:
Salutations to Devi Durga who slew the demon Raktabija and killed the demons, Chund and Mund.
O, Devi! Please grant me beauty, victory, glory, and destroy my enemies.

निशुम्भशुम्भनिर्नाशि त्रैलोक्यशुभदे नमः ।
रूपं देहि जयं देहि यशो देहि द्विषो जहि ॥७॥

Nishumbha-Shumbha-Nirnashi Trailokya-Shubhade Namah |
Rupam Dehi Jayam Dehi Yasho Dehi Dvisso Jahi ||7||

Meaning 7:
Salutations to Devi Durga who destroyed the demons Nishumbha and Shumbha; Salutations to the Devi who bestows auspiciousness in the three worlds.
Devi! Please grant me beauty, victory, glory, and destroy my enemies.

वन्दिताङ्घ्रियुगे देवि सर्वसौभाग्यदायिनि ।
रूपं देहि जयं देहि यशो देहि द्विषो जहि ॥८॥

Vandita-Angghri-Yuge Devi Sarva-Saubhagya-Dayini |
Rupam Dehi Jayam Dehi Yasho Dehi Dvisso Jahi ||8||

Meaning 8:
All praise salutations to Devi Durga, who is the bestower of wellbeing and good fortune.
O, Devi! Please grant me beauty, victory, glory, and destroy my enemies.

अचिन्त्यरूपचरिते सर्वशत्रुविनाशिनि ।
रूपं देहि जयं देहि यशो देहि द्विषो जहि ॥९॥

Acintya-Ruupa-Charite Sarva-Shatru-Vinashini |
Rupam Dehi Jayam Dehi Yasho Dehi Dvisso Jahi ||9||

Meaning 9:
Salutations to Mother Goddess Durga, whose forms are beyond comprehension, and who destroys all enemies.
O, Devi! Please grant me beauty, victory, glory, and destroy my enemies.

नतेभ्यः सर्वदा भक्त्या चापर्णे दुरितापहे ।
रूपं देहि जयं देहि यशो देहि द्विषो जहि ॥१०॥

Natebhyah Sarvada Bhaktya Cha-Aparne Durita-Apahe |
Rupam Dehi Jayam Dehi Yasho Dehi Dvisso Jahi ||10||

Meaning 10:
Salutations to Devi Aparna (another name of Devi) to whom Her devotees always bow with devotion and who keeps away the devotees from sins,
O, Devi! Please grant me beauty, victory, glory, and destroy my enemies.

स्तुवद्भयो भक्तिपूर्वं त्वां चण्डिके व्याधिनाशिनि ।
रूपं देहि जयं देहि यशो देहि द्विषो जहि ॥११॥

Stuvadbhayo Bhakti-Purvam Tvam Canddike Vyadhi-Nashini |
Rupam Dehi Jayam Dehi Yasho Dehi Dvisso Jahi ||11||

Meaning 11:
Salutation to Devi Chandika, to those who pray Devi with their devotion, Chandika destroys their ailments and diseases.
O, Devi! Please grant me beauty, victory, glory, and destroy my enemies.

चण्डिके सततं युद्धे जयन्ति पापनाशिनि ।
रूपं देहि जयं देहि यशो देहि द्विषो जहि ॥१२॥

Candike Satatam Yuddhe Jayanti Papa-Nashini |
Rupam Dehi Jayam Dehi Yasho Dehi Dvisso Jahi ||12||

Meaning 12:
Salutations to Chandika Devi, who wins every battle, and who destroys all sins.
O, Devi! Please grant me beauty, victory, glory, and destroy my enemies.

देहि सौभाग्यमारोग्यं देहि देवि परं सुखम् ।
रूपं देहि जयं देहि यशो देहि द्विषो जहि ॥१३॥

Dehi Saubhagyam-Aarogyam Dehi Devi Param Sukham |
Rupam Dehi Jayam Dehi Yasho Dehi Dvisso Jahi ||13||

Meaning 13:
O Devi, please bestow on me prosperity and wellbeing, along with good health and freedom from diseases; O Devi, please give me the ultimate happiness.
O, Devi! Please grant me beauty, victory, glory, and destroy my enemies.

विधेहि देवि कल्याणं विधेहि विपुलां श्रियम् ।
रूपं देहि जयं देहि यशो देहि द्विषो जहि ॥१४॥

Vidhehi Devi Kalyanam Vidhehi Vipulam Shriyam |
Rupam Dehi Jayam Dehi Yasho Dehi Dvisso Jahi ||14||

Meaning 14:
O Devi, please give me a good fortune; O Devi, please give me abundant prosperity,
O Devi! Please grant me beauty, victory, glory, and destroy my enemies.

विधेहि द्विषतां नाशं विधेहि बलमुच्चकैः ।
रूपं देहि जयं देहि यशो देहि द्विषो जहि ॥१५॥

Vidhehi Dvisatam Nasham Vidhehi Balam-Uchakaih |
Rupam Dehi Jayam Dehi Yasho Dehi Dvisso Jahi ||15||

Meaning 15:
O Devi, Please put down all my enemies; O Devi, please give me great strength and power,
O Devi! Please grant me beauty, victory, glory, and destroy my enemies.

सुरासुरशिरोरत्ननिघृष्टचरणेऽम्बिके ।
रूपं देहि जयं देहि यशो देहि द्विषो जहि ॥१६॥

Sura-Asura-Shiro-Ratna-Nighrsta-Charane-Ambike |
Rupam Dehi Jayam Dehi Yasho Dehi Dvisso Jahi ||16||

Meaning 16:
Salutations to Ambika Devi, to whose feet the devas touch their Heads out of devotion, and to whose feet the heads of Asuras adorned with Jewels get subdued.
O Devi! Please grant me beauty, victory, glory, and destroy my enemies.

विद्यावन्तं यशस्वन्तं लक्ष्मीवन्तञ्च मां कुरु ।
रूपं देहि जयं देहि यशो देहि द्विषो जहि ॥१७॥

Vidyavantam Yashasvantam Lakssmiivantan cha Maam Kuru |
Rupam Dehi Jayam Dehi Yasho Dehi Dvisso Jahi ||17||

Meaning 17:
O Devi, please give me knowledge, glory, attributes of Lakshmi (wealth and beauty).
O Devi! Please grant me beauty, victory, glory, and destroy my enemies.

देवि प्रचण्डदोर्दण्डदैत्यदर्पनिषूदिनि ।
रूपं देहि जयं देहि यशो देहि द्विषो जहि ॥१८॥

Devi Prachanda-Dordanda-Daitya-Darpa-Nisudini |
Rupam Dehi Jayam Dehi Yasho Dehi Dvisso Jahi ||18||

Meaning 18:
Salutations to Devi Durga, Who destroys the mighty pride of the overly violent and powerful demons.
O Devi! Please grant me beauty, victory, glory, and destroy my enemies.

प्रचण्डदैत्यदर्पघ्ने चण्डिके प्रणताय मे ।

रूपं देहि जयं देहि यशो देहि द्विषो जहि ॥१९॥

Pracanda-Daitya-Darpa-Ghne Chanddike Pranataya Me |
Rupam Dehi Jayam Dehi Yasho Dehi Dvisso Jahi ||19||

Meaning 19:
My Salutations to Chandika Devi, who is the destroyer of the terrible demons with mighty pride,
O Devi! Please grant me beauty, victory, glory, and destroy my enemies.

चतुर्भुजे चतुर्वक्त्रसंस्तुते परमेश्वरि ।

रूपं देहि जयं देहि यशो देहि द्विषो जहि ॥२०॥

Caturbhuje Catur-Vaktra-Samstute Parameshvari |
Rupam Dehi Jayam Dehi Yasho Dehi Dvisso Jahi ||20||

Meaning 20:
Salutations to the supreme Goddess Devi Durga, to whom the four facet and four hands Lord Brahma worship.
O Devi! Please grant me beauty, victory, glory, and destroy my enemies.

कृष्णेन संस्तुते देवि शश्वद्भक्त्या सदाम्बिके ।

रूपं देहि जयं देहि यशो देहि द्विषो जहि ॥२१॥

Krsnnena Samstute Devi Shashvad-Bhaktyaa Sada-Ambike |
Rupam Dehi Jayam Dehi Yasho Dehi Dvisso Jahi ||21||

Meaning 21:
Salutations to the supreme Ambika Devi, who is always praised by Lord Krishna with a continuous flow of devotion.
O Devi! Please grant me beauty, victory, glory, and destroy my enemies.

हिमाचलसुतानाथसंस्तुते परमेश्वरि ।
रूपं देहि जयं देहि यशो देहि द्विषो जहि ॥२२॥

Himacala-Suta-Natha-Samstute Parameshvari |
Rupam Dehi Jayam Dehi Yasho Dehi Dvisso Jahi ||22||

Meaning 22:
Salutations to the Supreme Goddess Durga Devi, who is praised by the Lord of the daughter of the Himachal mountain (i.e. by Lord Shiva).
O Devi! Please grant me beauty, victory, glory, and destroy my enemies.

इन्द्राणीपतिसद्भावपूजिते परमेश्वरि ।
रूपं देहि जयं देहि यशो देहि द्विषो जहि ॥२३॥

Indranni-Pati-Sadbhava-Pujite Parameshvari |
Rupam Dehi Jayam Dehi Yasho Dehi Dvisso Jahi ||23||

Meaning 23:
Salutations to the Supreme Goddess Durga Devi, Who is worshipped with true devotion by the consort of Indrani (Deva Indra).
O Devi! Please grant me beauty, victory, glory, and destroy my enemies.

देवि भक्तजनोद्दामदत्तानन्दोदयेऽम्बिके ।
रूपं देहि जयं देहि यशो देहि द्विषो जहि ॥२४॥

Devi Bhakta-Jano ddaama-Datta-anando-udaye-Ambike |
Rupam Dehi Jayam Dehi Yasho Dehi Dvisso Jahi ||24||

Meaning 24:
Salutations to Ambika Devi, who gives rise to an upsurge of ultimate joy in the hearts of Her devotees.
O Devi! Please grant me beauty, victory, glory, and destroy my enemies.

भार्यां मनोरमां देहि मनोवृत्तानुसारिणीम् ।
रूपं देहि जयं देहि यशो देहि द्विषो जहि ॥२५॥

Bharya Manoramam Dehi Mano-Vrtta-Anusarinim |
Rupam Dehi Jayam Dehi Yasho Dehi Dvisso Jahi ||25||

Meaning 25:
O Durga Devi, please grant me a beautiful wife matching my thoughts and qualities,
O Devi! Please grant me beauty, victory, glory, and destroy my enemies.

तारिणि दुर्गसंसारसागरस्याचलोद्भवे ।
रूपं देहि जयं देहि यशो देहि द्विषो जहि ॥२६॥

Tarini Durga-Samsara-Sagarasya-Achalo udbhave |
Rupam Dehi Jayam Dehi Yasho Dehi Dvisso Jahi ||26||

Meaning 26:
Salutations to Devi Durga, who took birth from the mountain and who enables us to cross the difficult ocean of the worldly karmas (samsara)
O Devi! Please grant me beauty, victory, glory, and destroy my enemies.

इदं स्तोत्रं पठित्वा तु महास्तोत्र पठेन्नरः ।
सप्तशर्ती समाराध्य वरमाप्नोति दुर्लभम् ॥२७॥

Idam Stotram Pathitvaa Tu Mahastotra Patthen-Narah |
Saptashatim Sama-araadhya Varam-Aapnoti Durlabham ||27||

Meaning 27:
Having Read Argala Stotra, one should then read the great Stotra (the core text of Shaktism Durga Saptashati),
Argala Stotra is equally revered like the Saptashati; those who read this with devotion obtains the boons for difficult things.

॥ इति अर्गलास्तोत्रम् समाप्ति ॥
|| Argala Stotram End ||

Keelak
Stotram

Keelak Stotram

Keelak Strotam is dedicated to Saraswati and Her various forms.

There are 14 Slokas in this text.

Keelak Stotram Summary: Sloka 1-14: People doubted that one could accomplish anything by reciting the Devi Mahatmyam, which appears to have the killing of Demons.

When people had this apprehension, Lord Shiva summoned all three lokas and pinned the underlying principle of the Conscious form of Devi to all.

People understood that Devi Mahatmyam has spiritual significance where it purges the inauspiciousness from within.

Why Recite Keelak Stotram?

Doubts about own strength lead to confusion and defeat. Believing in self-strength is the key. The Keelak Stotram clears the doubt and praises that when people had similar doubts, Lord Shiva cleared them all and demonstrated the importance of the divine mother, Shakti.

ऐश्वर्यं तत्प्रसादेन सौभाग्यारोग्यसम्पदः।
शत्रुहानिः परो मोक्षः स्तूयते सा न किं जनैः॥

Aishvaryam Tatprasadena Saubhagya-arogya-sampadah |
Shatruhanih Paro Mokshah Stuyate Sa Na Kim Janaih ||

जिनके प्रसाद से ऐश्वर्य, सौभाग्य, आरोग्य, सम्पत्ति, शत्रुनाश तथा परम मोक्ष की भी सिद्धि होती है, उन कल्याणमयी जगदम्बा की स्तुति मनुष्य क्यों नहीं करते? ॥

The Jagadamba, by whose grace divine qualities (Aishwaryam) are awakened, by whose presence good fortune (Saubhagya), health (freedom from disease - Arogya and wealth (Sampada) are manifested. By whose merciless enemies are eradicated, by whose grace one finally attains the highest liberation (Moksha); Why shouldn't the Devi be praised by the people (Who is all-merciful)?

|| कीलकस्तोत्रम् ||

|| Keelak Stotram ||

(Sanskrit Stotra and Meaning)

From Devi Mahatmayam (This text is recited before the Devi Mahatmayam core text)

ॐ अस्य श्रीकीलकमन्त्रस्य, शिव ऋषिः, अनुष्टुप् छन्दः, श्रीमहासरस्वती देवता,
श्रीजगदम्बाप्रीत्यर्थं सप्तशतीपाठाङ्गत्वेन जपे विनियोगः।
ॐ नमश्चण्डिकायै

OM Asya Shrikilakamantrasya ShivarIshih, Anushtup Chandah,
Shrimahasarasvati Devata, Shrijagadambaprityartham
Saptashatipatha Ngatvena Jape Viniyogah |
OM Namashchandikayai |

Om, let us recite Keelak Stotra, Rishi – Shiva, Chandah - Anushtup, Devata – Sri Maha Saraswati. These 700 slokas (known as Durga Saptsathi) are dedicated to Goddess Jagadamba. Salutation to Devi Chandika, who is another form of mother Goddess Jagdamba.

मार्कण्डेय उवाच

विशुद्धज्ञानदेहाय त्रिवेदीदिव्यचक्षुषे ।

श्रेयः प्राप्तिनिमित्ताय नमः सोमार्धधारिणे ॥१॥

Maarkannddeya Uvacaa
Vishuddha-Jnyaana-Dehaaya Tri-Vedi-Divya-Cakshuse |
Shreyah Prapti-Nimittaya Namah Soma-Ardha-Dharine ||1||

Meaning 1:

Markandeya Rishi said:

(I worship to Devi) The one who provides the absolute knowledge of three Vedas (Tri - Vedi) formed by Her three divine eyes.

Saluation to the Ardhanarishwar – half man and half woman (the Shiva and Shakti – who form this universe), the one who gives the good fortune.

Commentary:

Shiva is never changing, eternal, pure consciousness. Shakti is his energy or kinetic power. The universe is a manifestation of this energy.

सर्वमेतद् विजानीयान्मन्त्राणामपि कीलकम् ।

सोऽपि क्षेममवाप्नोति सततं जाप्यतत्परः ॥२॥

Sarvametad Vijaniyan-Mantranam-Api Kilakam |
So-Api Kshsemam-Avapnoti Satatam Japya-Tatparah ||2||

Meaning 2:

All the slokas part of Keelak Strotram are indeed Keelak in nature.

Whoever dedicates himself/herself to the continuous Japa (Chanting) of the Keelak Stotram attains the tranquillity of mind.

Commentary:

Keel means pin or nail, here Keelak means very focused mantras that pin down the underlying reality of Mother Goddess.

The tranquility of mind is a meditative state which is free from stress, anxiety, and depression.

सिद्ध्यन्त्युच्चाटनादीनि कर्माणि सकलान्यपि ।
एतेन स्तुवतां देविं स्तोत्रवृन्देन भक्तितः ॥३॥

Siddhyanty-Uccatana-adini Karmani Sakalanyi-Api |
Etena Stuvatam Devim Stotra-Vrndena Bhaktitah ||3||

Meaning 3:

The one who eradicates all inner enemies (desires, anger, deceit, ego, etc.) from their roots,
by worshiping the Devi with full dedication with all the mantras of Keelak Stotram.

Commentary:

In the spiritual sense, we have inner enemies like anger, ego, stress, anxiety, boundless desires, and many more. One can eradicate all the inner enemies by continuous chant of Devi Mantras with his full devotion.

न मन्त्रो नौषधं तत्र न किञ्चिदपि विद्यते ।
विना जप्येन सिद्ध्येत्तु सर्वमुच्चाटनादिकम् ॥४॥

Na Mantro Na-Ausadham Tatra Na Kincid-Api Vidyate |
Vina Japyena Siddhayet-Tu Sarvam-Uccaatana-Aadikam ||4||

Meaning 4:

No Mantras or medicine or even a trace of any can help
Without the recitation of Japa of Devi, one can not eradicate the enemies within.

Commentary:

This Mantra states one has to recite all the Mantras dedicated to Devi to achieve tranquillity of mind (a meditative state of mind which is free from stress, anxiety, and depression).

समग्राण्यपि सेत्स्यन्ति लोकशङ्कामिमां हरः ।
कृत्वा निमन्त्रयामास सर्वमेवमिदं शुभम् ॥५॥

Samagranny-Api Setsyanti Loka-Shangkam-Imam Harah |
Krtva Nimantrayamasa Sarvam-Evam-Idam Shubham ||5||

Meaning 5:
People had this apprehension that how everything is accomplished (by worshipping Mother Goddess Shakti and her Chandika Paath known as Devi Mahatymam),
(Lord Shiva summoned the representatives of all 3 Lokas) by inviting all (Shiva explained the underlying reality of Devi), and everything became auspicious.

Commentary:
When Deva and Asura went into a battle, Deva went to Lord Shiva, who invoked the Mother Goddess Shakti. The people had a doubt that how come a soft-hearted Devi will win this battle, so Lord Shiva explained the various fierce forms of Devi capable of killing all demons. People were satisfied with Shiva, and finally, the battle was won by Devi.

स्तोत्रं वै चण्डिकायास्तु तच्च गुह्यं चकार सः ।

समाप्नोति स पुण्येन तां यथावन्निमन्त्रणाम् ॥६॥

Stotram Vai Candikayastu Tacca Guhyam Cakara Sah |
Samapnoti Sa Punyena Tam Yathavan-Nimantranam ||6||

Meaning 6:
The Stotra of Devi Chandika (a form of Mother Goddess Shakti), has a deep hidden meaning and purpose (made by Lord Shiva),
Whoever invokes these Mantras in the prescribed manner, attains desired results.

Commentary:
Lord Shiva made the Goddess Shakti and its various forms. He understands all the forms and their purpose. When one understands the deep meaning behind each form, it's the spiritual significance and how to apply them in personal life certainly attain desired results.

सोऽपि क्षेममवाप्नोति सर्वमेव न संशयः ।

कृष्णायां वा चतुर्दश्यामष्टम्यां वा समाहितः ॥७॥

So-Api Kshemam-Avapnoti Sarvam-Eva Na Samshayah |
Krasnayam Va Caturdashyam-Ashtamyam Va Samahitah ||7||

Meaning 7:

There is no confusion that one attains the tranquillity of mind and all desired results, the one who worship Mother Goddess Shakti on Krishna Paksha Chaturdashi or Ashtami of a Vedic month.

Commentary:

There are specific days prescribed for the worship of mother Goddess Shakti. Those who pray on these days with full devotion attain the desired results.

ददाति प्रतिगृह्णाति नान्यथैषा प्रसीदति ।

इत्थंरूपेण कीलेन महादेवेन कीलितम् ॥८॥

Dadati Pratigrhnati Na-Anyathaia-Essa Prasidati |
Ittham-Rupena Kilena Mahadevena Keelitam ||8||

Meaning 8:

One who devotes himself to the Devi attains the blessings of Her; otherwise, Devi is not pleased by simple worship or recitation of Mantras without Bhakti (devotion),
Like this kind of explanation, Lord Shiva (Mahadev), pinned (Keelak) the Mantras of Devi worship.

Commentary:

Lord Shiva explained the importance of Devi worship with full devotion. He explained that a simple mechanical recitation of various Mantras associated with Devi is not going to give any kind of result. One has to be sincere enough to understand the true spiritual meaning behind each Mantra and adopt this in their personal life.

यो निष्कीलां विधायैनां चण्डीं जपति नित्यशः ।

स सिद्धः स गणः सोऽथ गन्धर्वो जायते ध्रुवम् ॥९॥

Yo Niskilam Vidhayai-Enam Candim Japati Nityashah |
Sa Sidhah Sa Ganah Sotha Gandharvo Jayate Dhruvam ||9||

Meaning 9:

By constantly reciting the Candi Paath (Devi Mahatymam), one who unpins the Keelak Stotram makes Devi manifest,
He truly becomes an enlightened soul (known as Siddha), a Gana (a companion of Devi), and a Gandharva (a celestial musician).

Commentary:

One who constantly recites the Devi Mahatymam Mantras with full devotion realizes the true meaning behind each Mantra and how to apply it in personal life. After the constant practice of Mantras and adopting these in life, one attains the spiritual enlightenment and becomes a Siddha, Gana, and Gandharva.

न चैवापाटवं तस्य भयं क्वापि न जायते ।

नापमृत्युवशं याति मृते च मोक्षमाप्नुयात् ॥१०॥

Na Caia-Eva-Apatavam Tasya Bhayam Kvapi Na Jayate |
Na-Apa-Mrtyu-Vasham Yati Mrte Ca Moksham-Aapnuyat ||10||

Meaning 10:

One does not become affected by an ailment, and no trace of fear can rise,
No premature death can occur; one attains the Self-realization (Moksha).

Commentary:

Those who recite and understand the true meaning of Devi Mahatymam, are free of disease, fear, premature death, and attain Self-realization or Liberation.

ज्ञात्वा प्रारभ्य कुर्वीत ह्यकुर्वाणो विनश्यति ।

ततो ज्ञात्वैव सम्पूर्णमिदं प्रारभ्यते बुधैः ॥११॥

Jnyatva Prarabhya Kurvita Hya-Akurvano Vinashyati |
Tato Jnyatvaiva Sampurnam-Idam Prarabhyate Budhaih ||11||

Meaning 11:

One who understands the Keelakam Stotram first, then only he should begin reciting the Devi Mahatyamam; otherwise, he will not get the benefit of recitation.
One who understands this (right order of recitation), the learned man begins reciting mantras.

Commentary:

The Mantra is explaining very clearly that Keelak Stotram should be recited before the recitation of the Candi Paath (Devi Mahatymam). This is the correct order if not followed, then benefit won't be received.

सौभाग्यादि च यत्किञ्चिद् दृश्यते ललनाजने ।
तत्सर्वं तत्प्रसादेन तेन जप्यमिदं शुभम् ॥१२॥

Saubhagya-Adi Ca Yatkincid Drshyate Lalanajane |
Tat-Sarvam Tat-Prasadena Tena Japyam-Idam Shubham ||12||

Meaning 12:
The qualities of good fortune, beauty, appeal and the features that are seen in a woman,
All are due to the blessings of Her Grace (Devi); therefore, all women should chant the Stotram of Devi.

Commentary:
It is the Devi by whom blessings woman receive all their qualities. Therefore women should chant the Devi Stotram.

शनैस्तु जप्यमानेऽस्मिन् स्तोत्रे सम्पत्तिरुच्चकैः ।
भवत्येव समग्रापि ततः प्रारभ्यमेव तत् ॥१३॥

Shanaistu Japyamane-Asmin Stotre Sampattir-Uccakaih |
Bhavatya-Eva Samagra-Api Tatah Prarabhyam-Eva Tat ||13||

Meaning 13:
One who chants Devi Stotram without haste (with all his full devotion), attains prosperity and wealth,
One develops a sense of completeness, and therefore, one should start the practice of chanting Keelak Stotram.

Commentary:
Many times we chant mantras mechanically without any dedication. This kind of practice does not yield any results. One should chant mantras gently, understand it's deep spiritual meaning, and then the only one attains the wholeness (the union of the self with the universe).

ऐश्वर्यं यत्प्रसादेन सौभाग्यारोग्यसम्पदः ।
शत्रुहानिः परो मोक्षः स्तूयते सा न किं जनैः ॥१४॥

Aishvaryam Yat-Prasadena Saubhagya-Aarogya-Sampadah |
Shatru-Haniah Paro Mokshah Stuyate Sa Na Kim Janaih ||14||

Meaning 14:
By the whose grace one attains the qualities like Devas, good fortune, well being, and prosperity,
By whose grace one attains the destruction of enemies and Self-realization (Moksha), why such Devi be not worshipped by the people?

Commentary:
The Devi gives all the divine qualities, good fortune, well-being, wealth, eradication of enemies, and liberation from samsara. There is no reason why people should not pray to such a powerful and graceful Devi.

चण्डिकां हृदयेनापि यः स्मरेत् सततं नरः ।
हृद्यं काममवाप्नोति हृदि देवी सदा वसेत् ॥१५॥

Candikam Hrdayena-Api Yah Smaret Satatam Narah |
Hrdyam Kamam-Avapnoti Hrdi Devi Sada Vaset ||15||

Meaning 15:
One who constantly remembers the Mother Goddess Candi from his heart with full devotion,
He attains the innermost longing and desires, and the Devi always dwells in his heart.

Commentary:
The people who are regular in their practice of Devi worship with full devotion, Devi fulfills their innermost desires. Devi becomes their companion in their spiritual journey.

अग्रतोऽमुं महादेवकृतं कीलकवारणम् ।
निष्किलञ्च तथा कृत्वा पठितव्यं समाहितैः ॥१६॥

Agrato-Amum Mahadeva-Krtam Keelaka-Varanam |
Niskilanca Tatha Krtva Pathitavyam Samahitaih ||16||

Meaning 16:
First, Lord Shiva (Mahadev) created the Keelak Stotram,
and this Stotram should be unpinned, only after that one should recite the Devi Mahatymam.

Commentary:

Lord Shiva first described the importance of how to unpin the true meaning behind various forms of the Shakti. He showed the underlying reality of Shakti and how it manifests in various forms. He also gave a clear understanding of the spiritual significance of each form and how to adopt it in our life. Shiva described that chanting of these Mantras needs full devotion to realize the conscious form of Mother Goddess Shakti.

॥ इति कीलकस्तोत्रम् समाप्ति ॥
|| Keelak Stotram End ||

Devi Mahatymam

Durga Saptashati
700 Mantras of Markandeya Purana

The Markandeya Purana (मार्कण्डेय पुराण) is one among 108 Purana text of Hinduism. It is also one of the 18 classified Mahapurana text.

It has approx. 9000 verses and 137 chapters.
The 700 slokas of chapters 81 to 93 are dedicated to Mother Goddess Durga and her glories called "Devi Mahatmyam."

Durga Saptashati – 13 Chapters Details

Navaratri Day	Chapter	Story
1	1	Destruction of Madhu Kaitabha
2	2,3,4	Destruction of Mahiṣhasura
3	5,6	Slaying of Dhmmra-lochana
4	7	Slaying of Chaṇda Muṇda
5	8	Destruction of Rakta-bija
6	9,10	Slaying of Shumbha and Nishumbha
7	11	Hymn to Shri Narayani
8	12	Character of Devi's Forms
9	13	Boons to the King and business man

Durga Saptashati - Summary

Markaṇḍeya Rishi narrates the story to his disciple Bhaguri. He tells the story of Savarni, who is the son of Surya and known as eighth Manu.

In the svarochish manvantara, there was a king called Surath. He ruled the entire earth. He was from the Chaitra dynasty. His enemies, the Kola kings, defeated him and destroyed his kingdom. He took shelter in the hermitage of Medhas Rishi living outside the jungle. He also met a merchant named Samadhi, who lost his wealth to his family members and became penniless.

They both approached Medha Rishi. Medha Rishi gave them supreme knowledge about the creation. He explained this entire existence, and this universe is only possible when the Shakti takes a form called Mahamaya. Then he narrated the story of how, when Vishnu was in yoga nidra (deep sleep), two Asura (demons) Madhu and Kaiṭabha tried to kill Brahma. Brahma unable to defeat them worshipped to Devi, who came forward and woke up Vishnu from His deep sleep and then killed both Asura.

Durga Saptashati - Summary

Chapter 2-4: Markaṇḍeya Rishi continues narrating the glories of the Devi Shakti.

A long time ago, Mahishasura was the Lord of Asuras (Demons), and Indra was the Lord of Devas. Devas and Asuras fought a war that lasted full hundred years. Finally, the army of the Devas was defeated, and Mahishasura became the Lord of Heaven.

Devas had no power left so, they went to Shiva and Vishnu. Shiva and Vishnu created a female form called Shakti or Durga. All Devas and other Gods empowered Devi with their unique powers and weapons. Then started the battle between Devi Chandika and Mahishasura. Devi alone killed the entire army of Mahishasura and finally slew him too.

Chapter 5-10: Markaṇḍeya Rishi continues narrating the glories of the Devi Bhagavati, Jagadamba, and many other forms and how she continues to help Devas and Humans. She killed all Asuras like Dhumra-lochana, Chaṇḍa-Muṇḍa, Rakta-bija, and Shumbha-Nishumbha.

Chapter 11-12: Describes how Devas worshiped the Devi Narayani and various characters of Devi forms.

Chapter 13: In this final chapter, both the King Surath and Merchant Samadhi got boon and enlightenment.

Devi Durga 108 Names

Number	Durga Devi Name	English Meaning	मां दुर्गा के नाम	नाम का अर्थ
1	Sati	One who got burned alive	सती	अग्नि में जल कर भी जीवित होने वाली
2	Saadhvi	The Sanguine	साध्वी	आशावादी
3	Bhavaprita	One who is loved by the universe	भवप्रीता	भगवान शिव पर प्रीति रखने वाली
4	Bhavani	The abode of the universe	भवानी	ब्रहमांड में निवास करने वाली
5	Bhavamochani	The absolver of the universe	भवमोचनी	संसारिक बंधनों से मुक्त करने वाली
6	Aarya	Goddess	आर्या	देवी
7	Durga	The Invincible	दुर्गा	अपराजेय
8	Jaya	The Victorious	जया	विजयी
9	Aadya	The Initial reality	आद्य	शुरुआत की वास्तविकता
10	Trinetra	One who has three-eyes	त्रिनेत्र	तीन आंखों वाली
11	Shooldharini	One who holds a monodent	शूलधारिणी	शूल धारण करने वाली
12	Pinaakadharini	One who holds the trident of Shiva	पिनाकधारिणी	शिव का त्रिशूल धारण करने वाली
13	Chitra	The Picturesque	चित्रा	सुरम्य, सुंदर
14	Chandaghanta	One who has mighty bells	चण्डघण्टा	प्रचण्ड स्वर से घण्टा नाद करने वाली
15	Mahatapa	With severe penance	सुधा	अमृत की देवी
16	Manah	Mind	मन	मनन
17	Buddhi	Intelligence	बुद्धि	सर्वज्ञाता
18	Ahankaara	One with Pride	अहंकारा	अभिमान करने वाली
19	Chittarupa	One who is in thought-state	चित्तरूपा	वह जो सोच की अवस्था में है
20	Chita	Death-bed	चिता	मृत्युशय्या
21	Chiti	The thinking mind	चिति	चेतना
22	Sarvamantramayi	One who possess all the instruments of thought	सर्वमन्त्रमयी	सभी मंत्रों का ज्ञान रखने वाली
23	Satta	One who is above all	सत्ता	सत
24	Satyanandasvarupini	Form of Eternal bliss	सत्यानंद स्वरूपिणी	अनन्त आनंद का रूप
25	Ananta	One who is Infinite or beyond measure	अनन्ता	जिनके स्वरूप का कहीं अंत नहीं
26	Bhaavini	The Beautiful Woman	भाविनी	सबको उत्पन्न करने वाली, खूबसूरत औरत
27	Bhaavya	Represents Future	भाव्या	भावना एवं ध्यान करने योग्य
28	Bhavya	With Magnificence	भव्या	कल्याणरूपा, भव्यता के साथ
29	Abhavya	Improper or fear-causing	अभव्या	जिससे बढ़कर भव्य कुछ नहीं
30	Sadagati	Always in motion, bestowing Moksha (salvation)	सदागति	हमेशा गति में, मोक्ष दान
31	Shaambhavi	Consort of Shambhu	शाम्भवी	शिवप्रिया, शंभू की पत्नी
32	Devamata	Mother Goddess	देवमाता	देवगण की माता
33	Chinta	Tension	चिन्ता	चिन्ता
34	Ratnapriya	Adorned or loved by jewels	रत्नप्रिया	गहने से प्यार करने वाली
35	Sarvavidya	Knowledgeable	सर्वविद्या	ज्ञान का निवास
36	Dakshakanya	Daughter of Daksha	दक्षकन्या	दक्ष की बेटी

Devi Durga 108 Names

Num ber	Durga Devi Name	English Meaning	मां दुर्गा के नाम	नाम का अर्थ
37	Dakshayajñavinaashini	Interrupter of the sacrifice of Daksha	दक्षयज्ञविनाशिनी	दक्ष के यज्ञ को रोकने वाली
38	Aparna	One who doesn't eat even leaves while fasting	अपर्णा	तपस्या के समय पत्ते को भी न खाने वाली
39	Anekavarna	One who has many complexions	अनेकवर्णा	अनेक रंगों वाली
40	Paatala	Red in color	पाटला	लाल रंग वाली
41	Paatalavati	Wearing red-color attire	पाटलावती	गुलाब के फूल
42	Pattaambaraparidhaana	Wearing a dress made of leather	पट्टाम्बरपरीधाना	रेशमी वस्त्र पहनने वाली
43	Kalamanjiiraranjini	Wearing a musical anklet	कलामंजीरारंजिनी	पायल को धारण करके प्रसन्न रहने वाली
44	Ameyaa	One who is beyond measure	अमेय	जिसकी कोई सीमा नहीं
45	Vikrama	Violent	विक्रमा	असीम पराक्रमी
46	Krrooraa	Brutal (on demons)	क्रूरा	दैत्यों के प्रति कठोर
47	Sundari	The Gorgeous	सुन्दरी	सुंदर रूप वाली
48	Sursundari	Extremely Beautiful	सुरसुन्दरी	अत्यंत सुंदर
49	Vandurga	Goddess of forests	वनदुर्गा	जंगलों की देवी
50	Maatangi	Goddess of Matanga	मातंगी	मतंगा की देवी
51	Matangamunipujita	Worshipped by Sage Matanga	मातंगमुनिपूजिता	बाबा मतंगा द्वारा पूजनीय
52	Braahmi	Power of God Brahma	ब्राह्मी	भगवान ब्रह्मा की शक्ति
53	Maaheshvari	Power of Lord Mahesha (Shiva)	माहेश्वरी	प्रभु शिव की शक्ति
54	Aeindri	Power of God Indra	इंद्री	इंद्र की शक्ति
55	Kaumaari	The adolescent	कौमारी	किशोरी
56	Vaishnavi	The invincible	वैष्णवी	अजेय
57	Chaamunda	Slayer of Chanda and Munda(demons)	चामुण्डा	चंड और मुंड का नाश करने वाली
58	Varahi	One who rides on Varaah	वाराही	वराह पर सवार होने वाली
59	Lakshmi	Goddess of Wealth	लक्ष्मी	सौभाग्य की देवी
60	Purushaakriti	One who takes the form of a man	पुरुषाकृति	वह जो पुरुष धारण कर ले
61	Vimalauttkarshini	One who provides joy	विमिलौत्त्कार्शिनी	आनन्द प्रदान करने वाली
62	Gyaana	Full of Knowledge	ज्ञाना	ज्ञान से भरी हुई
63	Kriya	One who is in action	क्रिया	हर कार्य में होने वाली
64	Nitya	The eternal one	नित्या	अनन्त
65	Buddhida	The bestower of wisdom	बुद्धिदा	ज्ञान देने वाली
66	Bahula	One who is in various forms	बहुला	विभिन्न रूपों वाली
67	Bahulaprema	One who is loved by all	बहुलप्रेमा	सर्व प्रिय
68	Sarvavahanavahana	One who rides all vehicles	सर्ववाहनवाहना	सभी वाहन पर विराजमान होने वाली
69	NishumbhaShumbhaHanani	Slayer of the demon-brothers	निशुम्भशुम्भहननी	शुम्भ, निशुम्भ का वध करने वाली
70	MahishasuraMardini	Slayer of the bull-demon Mahishaasura	महिषासुरमर्दिनि	महिषासुर का वध करने वाली
71	MadhuKaitabhaHantri	Slayer of the demon-duo Madhu and Kaitabha	मसुकैटभहंत्री	मधु व कैटभ का नाश करने वाली
72	ChandaMundaVinashini	Destroyer of the ferocious asuras Chanda and Munda	चण्डमुण्ड विनाशिनी	चंड और मुंड का नाश करने वाली

Devi Durga 108 Names

Number	Durga Devi Name	English Meaning	मां दुर्गा के नाम	नाम का अर्थ
73	Sarvasuravinasha	Destroyer of all demons	सर्वासुरविनाशा	सभी राक्षसों का नाश करने वाली
74	Sarvadaanavaghaatini	Possessing the power to kill all the demons	सर्वदानवघातिनी	संहार के लिए शक्ति रखने वाली
75	Satya	The truth	सत्या	सच्चाई
76	Sarvaastradhaarini	Possessor of all the missile weapons	सर्वास्त्रधारिणी	सभी हथियारों धारण करने वाली
77	Anekashastrahasta	Possessor of many hand weapons	अनेकशस्त्रहस्ता	कई हथियार धारण करने वाली
78	AnekastraDhaarini	Possessor of many weapons	अनेकास्त्रधारिणी	अनेक हथियारों को धारण करने वाली
79	Kumaari	The beautiful adolescent	कुमारी	सुंदर किशोरी
80	Ekakanya	The girl child	एककन्या	कन्या
81	Kaishori	The adolescent	कैशोरी	जवान लड़की
82	Yuvati	The Woman	युवती	नारी
83	Yati	Ascetic, one who renounces the world	यति	तपस्वी
84	Apraudha	One who never gets old	अप्रौढा	जो कभी पुराना ना हो
85	Praudha	One who is old	प्रौढा	जो पुराना है
86	Vriddhamaata	The old mother (loosely)	वृद्धमाता	शिथिल
87	Balaprada	The bestower of strength	बलप्रदा	शक्ति देने वाली
88	Mahodari	One who has huge belly which stores the universe	महोदरी	ब्रह्मांड को संभालने वाली
89	Muktakesha	One who has open tresses	मुक्तकेशी	खुले बाल वाली
90	Ghorarupa	Having a fierce outlook	घोररूपा	एक भयंकर दृष्टिकोण वाली
91	Mahaabala	Having immense strength	महाबला	अपार शक्ति वाली
92	Agnijwaala	One who is poignant like fire	अग्निज्वाला	मार्मिक आग की तरह
93	Raudramukhi	One who has a fierce face like destroyer Rudra	रौद्रमुखी	विध्वंसक रुद्र की तरह भयंकर चेहरा
94	Kaalaratri	Goddess who is black like night	कालरात्रि	काले रंग वाली
95	Tapasvini	one who is engaged in penance	तपस्विनी	तपस्या में लगे हुए
96	Narayani	The destructive aspect of Lord Narayana	नारायणी	भगवान नारायण की विनाशकारी रूप
97	Bhadrakaali	Fierce form of Kali	भद्रकाली	काली का भयंकर रूप
98	Vishnumaya	Spell of Lord Vishnu	विष्णुमाया	भगवान विष्णु का जादू
99	Jalodari	Abode of the ethereal universe	जलोदरी	ब्रह्मांड में निवास करने वाली
100	Shivadooti	Ambassador of Lord Shiva	शिवदूती	भगवान शिव की राजदूत
101	Karaali	The Violent	करली	हिंसक
102	Ananta	The Infinite	अनन्ता	विनाश रहित
103	Parameshvari	The Ultimate Goddess	परमेश्वरी	प्रथम देवी
104	Katyayani	One who is worshipped by sage Katyanan	कात्यायनी	ऋषि कात्यायन द्वारा पूजनीय
105	Savitri	Daughter of the Sun	सावित्री	सूर्य की बेटी
106	Pratyaksha	One who is real	प्रत्यक्षा	वास्तविक
107	Brahmavaadini	One who is present everywhere	ब्रह्मवादिनी	वर्तमान में हर जगह वास करने वाली
108	Sarvashaastramayi	One who is deft in all theories	सर्वशास्त्रमयी	सभी सिद्धांतों में निपुण

Navaratri Stories

Day 1

Shailaputri

On the first day of Navratri, we worship a form of Shakti called Shailaputri. Goddess Shakti represents a pure, divine female power. In Sanskrit, 'Shail' means mountain, and 'Putri' means daughter. Together they mean "daughter of the mountain." This is the legend of Shailaputri.

This story starts with Brahma, the creator, and his son, Kama, the God of love. Kama's wife, Rati, was the Goddess of love. Brahma had observed the Gods for some time. Brahma noticed how he and Saraswati were married and how Vishnu and Lakshmi were married. He could not help but worry for his single friend, Shiva. Brahma thought that getting Shiva married would benefit the universe. So, Brahma had Kama and Rati use their powers of love to arrange a marriage for Shiva. Simple, right? Nope, not at all.

All of Kama and Rati's attempts failed. Some of their acts were so extreme that they enraged Shiva. One attempt as such infuriated Shiva, which leads him to incinerate the Kama from his eye. Shiva always said that he was a yogin. He was meant to stay away from these worldly things.

Running out of ideas to get his friend married, Brahma resorted to praying and worshipping Goddess Shakti. Goddess Shakti was pleased with Brahma and offered him one boon. He asked her to take birth in this world in hopes of marrying Shiva. She agreed to this.

Brahma was overjoyed with the news. He promptly informed his son, King Daksha, of the news and urged him to carry out a penance. After hundreds of years of praying and worshipping, the Goddess presented herself before Daksha and his wife. She was pleased with them and offered them a boon. Daksha asked her to take birth into his world as his daughter. The Goddess complied. However, she warned Daksha that if he were ever to disrespect her, then she would leave this world. Thinking nothing of it, Daksha rejoiced.

A few years passed, and Daksha's wife gave birth to the Goddess. They celebrated her coming into their world with joy and called her Sati. During her childhood, Sage Narada and Brahma came to visit her in the palace. They reminded Sati of why she came to this world and her mission to marry Shiva. Years later, Sati decided to carry out a penance. Sati was an extremely dedicated woman. Gods and Sages came to watch her. They were blown away by her extreme focus and passion.

One day, the Gods and sages who were examining Sati decided to visit Shiva in Mount Kailash. They praised Shiva. Brahma suggested that he marry someone. Upon hearing this, Shiva sighed. He told them that he was a Yogin. Shiva explained that yogins should be detached from these things. He finally agreed to marry under the conditions that his wife would be loving and a yogini.

Brahma spoke of Sati, a beautiful girl who was loving and executing a penance. After some persuasion, Shiva accepted the idea. This satisfied all the Gods and Sages.

Meanwhile, Sati was still executing her penance. Shiva observed Sati, and he, too, was appalled by her devotion. He appeared before Sati and extended her one boon. Sati asked for them to get married. Shiva granted the boon, and the pair got happily married in Daksha's palace.

A few years later, Brahma planned a grand yagna with lots of guests, including Shiva and Sati. When Daksha arrived at the event, every soul bowed down to him. The only people who did not bow down to Daksha were Brahma and Shiva. Brahma was Daksha's father, so it made sense for him to stay standing. Shiva was of a higher position than Brahma, so it also made sense for Shiva to stay standing. However, Daksha had other ideas. He thought that his son-in-law Shiva was insulting him by staying standing. This provoked Daksha. In a fit of rage, Daksha cursed Shiva. Nandi became enraged and began to retaliate when Shiva intervened and assured everyone that he had not been cursed. Everyone began to leave. Daksha returned home with a newfound grudge.

A while later, Sati noticed that people were traveling to an event. After inquiring, Sati realized that there was a yagna taking place and being hosted by none other than her father, Daksha. Sati rushed home and told Shiva about her father's yagna and how they were not invited. Sati was very irritated, but she also missed her family very much. She decided that she would go to the yagna.

At the yagna, Sati's mother and sister greeted her. However, her father continuously ignored her presence. This annoyed Sati, and she began preaching how no yagna could be complete without Shiva. Daksha proceeded to insult Sati and Shiva. Hearing Daksha insult her family was unbearable for Sati. She was horrified that Daksha also broke their agreement. Sati became so humiliated that she threw herself into the sacrificial fire.

Shiva's Ganas explained the painful death of Sati to him. From his hair, Shiva created two forms, Virabhadra and Bhadrakali, and ordered them to destroy the yagna. Virabhadra got carried away and decapitated Daksha and killed others. After the horrific event, Shiva resuscitated those who died and gave them blessings. Shiva revived Daksha replacing the decapitated head with the sacrificed sheep's head. Daksha apologized to Shiva and spent the rest of his years as a devotee of Shiva.

Grief-stricken Shiva carried Sati's body around the universe, recollecting their memories. Vishnu cut Sati's body into 51 parts, which fell on the earth. The spots where the parts landed became holy sites people prayed to the Goddess. These 51 sites are called Shakti Peethas.

Shiva became miserable. He retreated to the mountains and meditated. The Gods noticed Shiva's grief and thought of ways to help him.

At the same time, a powerful asura, Tarakasura, had shown himself. Tarakasura had a blessing that he could only be killed by Shiva's son. This frightened the Gods as Shiva did not have a son, and his wife had just passed away.

They decided to pray to Goddess Shakti again. They wanted to remind her of her form, Sati, who had been married to Shiva. They asked her to take birth in their world again. She agreed to be born again, this time as the daughter of Himavan and Menavati. Himavan and Mena performed penance for a long time. The Goddess gave them a boon, and they asked for the Goddess to take birth as their daughter.

Soon enough, Mena gave birth to the Goddess. She was named Parvati. Since Parvati was the daughter of the Himavan, she is known as 'Shailaputri.'

Navaratri Stories

Day 2

Brahmacharini

On the second day of Navratri, we worship Maa Brahmacharini. In Sanskrit, 'Brahma' means penance, and 'Charini' means a female follower.

Following Sati's death, Shiva had retreated into the mountains. During this time, the Gods were being attacked by the asuras. The asuras were led by Tarakasura, who had a boon that only Shiva's son could kill him. The Gods were worried because Shiva's wife, Sati, had just died. Shiva had no children. As long as Shiva had no children, Tarakasura would be a threat.

The Gods prayed to Goddess Shakti and convinced her to take birth in their world again. They also asked her to marry Shiva again. Goddess Shakti was born to Himavan and Mena. She was called Parvati or Shailaputri.

During her childhood, Sage Narada visited Parvati. He reminded Parvati of her past life as Sati. He told her that there was still a chance for her to marry Shiva if she carried out penances. Parvati became determined to marry Shiva in this birth as well. A few years later, Parvati got her parents' permission and set off to execute a penance.

Parvati's penance was extreme and full of devotion. Her penance lasted thousands of years. She resided on the ground in a forest, and she wore ordinary clothes. For the first thousand years, Parvati survived eating fruits and berries. For the next hundred years, she only ate vegetables. She then ate the leaves on the ground. Soon after, she stopped eating altogether. After Parvati stopped eating leaves, she became known as Aparna. Aparna means 'without leaves' in Sanskrit.

Parvati's mother became distraught when she saw the harsh conditions her daughter was living in. When she saw Parvati, she exclaimed, "O! Ma!". People began to refer to Parvati as 'Uma' as well. The rumor of a severe and strict penance spread around. Eventually, Brahma appeared before Parvati. He told her that no one had ever seen such a penance. This is how Parvati got the name Tapascharini or Brahmacharini.

Brahma then visited Shiva in Mount Kailash. He told Shiva about Parvati's penance. He asked Shiva to be merciful and to marry Parvati. Shiva decided to see Parvati. Shiva presented himself to Parvati in a hidden form. He pretended to be a wandering man and repeatedly insulted Shiva. Parvati protected Shiva. Shiva could feel her devotion towards him. He was extremely pleased. Shiva revealed his proper form to her and gave her a boon, and they became engaged.

Navaratri Stories

Day 3

Chandraghanta

On the third day of Navratri, we worship a form of Goddess Shakti called Ma Chandraghanta.

After Sati died, Shiva went into a deep meditation in the mountains. During this time, a powerful asura, Tarakasura, showed himself. The Gods feared him because he had a boon that only Shiva's son could kill him. To ease their fears, the Gods prayed to Goddess Shakti and asked her to take birth in their world again. They asked her to marry Shiva once again. Goddess Shakti was born to Himavan and Mena. They called her Parvati. Parvati carried out a deep penance which pleased Shiva. The pair decided to get married.

On the day of the wedding, Parvati's mother had been excitedly waiting for the groom. She pointed at nearly every male who entered Himavan's palace and asked for their name. Eventually, when Sage Narada pointed out who Shiva was, Mena fainted from shock. Shiva had come to the venue in a terrorizing form. He had ash smeared all over his body and lots of snakes wrapped around him as well. His marriage procession included ganas, ghosts, sages and ascetics. Many other guests fainted as well.

When Mena woke up, she began crying and cursing everyone in the room. She could not bear the thought of her daughter marrying such a terrifying being.

Parvati did not want her family or Shiva to feel embarrassed. Parvati transformed herself into a petrifying form called Chandraghanta. In this form, Parvati prayed to Shiva and begged him to change his form into a more lavish one. She asked him to dress up his marriage procession as well.

Shiva and his marriage procession appeared before everyone else again- this time much richer and suitably. Shiva looked like a handsome prince and wore many jewels. We celebrate the wedding of Shiva and Parvati each year on Mahashivratri.

Navaratri Stories

Day 4

Kushmanda

On the fourth day of Navratri, we worship the form of Goddess Shakti, Ma Kushmanda. In Sanskrit, 'Ku' means little, 'Usha' means energy, and 'Anda' means egg. Together it means 'little cosmic eggs.'

The story of Ma Kushmanda goes a long way back. It goes back to way before the universe even existed. In the Puranas, it states that Ma Kushmanda smiled. From her smile, a 'little cosmic egg' was produced. The 'little cosmic egg' refers to divine energy. This energy created the universe.

Not only did Ma Kushmanda create the universe. She also created the first beings. She created three cosmic Goddesses. From her left eye, she created a frightening form called

Mahakali. She created an intimidating form called Mahalakshmi from her center eye. Lastly, from her right eye, Kushmanda created a lavish form called Mahasaraswati.

From the body of Mahakali, two beings took birth. One was Shiva, and the other was called Saraswati. The same thing happened to Mahalakshmi and Mahasaraswati. The two beings who took birth from Mahalakshmi's body were called Brahma and Lakshmi. Finally, the beings that emerged from Mahalakshmi were called Vishnu and Shakti. Brahma, Shiva, and Vishnu make up the Trideva while Lakshmi, Saraswati, and Shakti make up the Tridevi.

It is believed that Ma Kushmanda absorbed the three cosmic Goddesses and entered Shakti. Thus, we worship her as a form of Shakti.

Navaratri Stories

Day 5

Skandmata

The fifth day of the Hindu Festival Navratri is celebrated in honor of Goddess Skandamata, who is the Fifth avatar of Durga.

Goddess Skandamata is another name for Parvati, who is originally Sati. Sati was Lord Shiva's first spouse. After Sati's death, Lord Shiva had gone into a deep meditation. At the time, the Gods were being attacked by demons that were being led by demons, Tarakasura, and Surapadman. Tarakasura and Surapadman had asked Bramha for a boon, that only the son of Lord Shiva could defeat them, so they had to bring Sati back as Parvati and make Lord Shiva fall in love with her, for their son to be born, and kill the demons Surapadman and Tarakasura. When Sati had been reborn as Parvati, Sage Narada had come to Parvati to tell her about

her previous life as Sati and told her the purpose of her rebirth. However, to get Lord Shiva to notice her, and recognize she was Sati, Parvati had to perform severe penance.

Years had gone by, but Lord Shiva did not take notice of Parvati, and the demons were getting stronger by the day. The Gods were troubled by this, so they decided to get God Manmat, (God of Love) to use his powers and get Lord Shiva to fall in love with Parvati again, and Manmat agreed. When Lord Shiva awoke from his deep meditation, he saw that Manmat had disturbed him and burnt him to ashes. However, his powers had worked, and he had noticed Parvati performing penance for him. Soon after, Lord Shiva had fallen in love with Parvati and married her, and that was when their energies had combined to create the seed of their son. Agni, the God of fire, was entrusted to carry it to a lake in Forest Saravana, (which means 'Forest of Reeds') but could not bear any longer, so he passed it on to Ganga, who securely brought it to Forest Saravana. There, he handed the seed to six sisters known as 'Krittikas', and soon enough, became a baby boy, son of Lord Shiva and Goddess Parvati. As he was cared for by 'Krittikas' he had been named 'Kartikeya'. Kartikeya had another name, 'Skand', which has many meanings, including 'effuse'. Therefore, Parvati was given the name 'Skandamata', meaning the 'mother of Skand'. Thus, Kartikeya or Skand went on and eliminated Tarakasura and Surapadman, along with all the demons that followed, and bring peace to the Gods.

On the fifth day of Navratri, the Goddess is worshipped in the form of Skandmata, as she proved essential in the process of restoring the peace.

Navaratri Stories

Day 6

Katyayani

There was a sage named Katyayan, who was a dedicated follower of Goddess Shakti. His greatest wish was for her to be born as his daughter and prayed endlessly for his wish to be granted. Meanwhile, a demon called Mahishasura, who was part Water Buffalo, was growing stronger by the day, which distressed the Gods.

The Gods decided to pray to Goddess Shakti, hoping she could somehow defeat him. So, Goddess Shakti decided to come to earth to discipline Mahishasura. Of course, she chose to be born as the daughter of Sage Katyayan and came to be

called Katyayani, and Katyayani grew up to become a beautiful young lady.

One day, two of Mahishasura's messengers spotted Katyayani and thought that she and Mahishasura would make a great match, so they reported this to Mahishasura. Mahishasura then sent one of his messengers to Katyayani. The messenger told her how powerful Mahishasura was and said that they would make a great couple. Katyayani agreed, but she said that she had to follow a family tradition that she could only marry Mahishasura if he defeated her in battle. The messenger then went back and told Mahishasura what she had said, and preparations for the battle began immediately.

When the battle had begun, Katyayani noticed that an army of demons accompanied Mahishasura in battle, but she slew most of them anyway. After, there were a few that were harder to kill, so she then took care of them. She then battled Mahishasura, who was quite tough to fight and had just turned into a Water Buffalo, so Katyayani climbed on his back, and he had trouble shaking her off. She held him down with her foot and pierced him with her trident, that was gifted to her by Lord Shiva. Once again, she brought peace to earth and the Gods. On the sixth day of Navratri, she is worshipped as Katyayani.

Navaratri Stories

Day 7

Kalaratri

The seventh day of Navratri is dedicated to Goddess Kalaratri, the seventh form of Durga.

Two demons named Shumbh and Nishumbh, who had a brother named Namuchi who was killed by Indra. Shumbh and Nishumbh were enraged and decided to attack the Gods in order to avenge him. Demons called Chanda, Munda and Raktabeej, (who were messengers and friends of Mahishasura before Kaytayani defeated him), had joined Shumbh and Nishumbh. Together, they attacked the Gods and took over the three worlds. The Gods prayed to Goddess Shakti for help, so she transformed into Goddess Kaushiki, and invited Shumbh and Nishumbh to a battle. They brought a mob of demons with them, but Kaushiki's glare slew most of them, but others like Chanda, Munda, and Raktabeej were more powerful.

To help her fight all the demons, she created another Goddess, Goddess Kali or Kaalaratri. Kaalaratri fought ruthlessly and killed the other more powerful demons quickly, but Chanda and Munda had fled the battlefield. Kaalaratri went after the two, cut off their heads, and wore their heads as a headdress, which came to be known as Chamunda.

Kalaratri then went on and fought the other demons, while Kaushiki battled Raktabeej, who had power. Every time he bled and a drop of blood touched the ground; a demon-like Raktabeej arose once again. Raktabeej proved quite troublesome, so Kaushiki called Kaalaratri to help fight him. Whenever Kaushiki struck Raktabeej, Kaalaratri drank his blood without letting it fall to the ground. They eventually defeated Raktabeej, Shumbh, and Nishumbh, and saved the Gods. This is the story of Goddess Kalaratri.

Navaratri Stories

Day 8

Mahaguari

On the eighth day of Navratri, we worship the form of Goddess Shakti called Mahagauri.

Mahagauri translates to too white or fair.
This story begins after Sati threw herself in the sacrificial fire and was reborn as Parvati. When Parvati was young, Sage Narada visited her and reminded her of her quest to marry Shiva. He advised her to perform a penance. With her parents' permission, 16-year-old Parvati set off to start her penance.

Parvati slept on the forest floor under the open sky for thousands of years. She was exposed to harsh sun rays, rain, and storms. On top of that, Parvati's diet consisted of nothing. Due to this, Parvati became so skinny she resembled a twig. Her once fair complexion had turned dark and dirty.

Shiva disguised himself and appeared before Parvati. He was pleased with her and agreed to marry her. Shiva used the water from the Ganges stored in the locks of his hair to bathe Parvati in it. He washed her until her complexion and clothes glowed radiantly.

In this form, Mahagauri rode a white bull and dressed in white. Therefore, she is called Mahagauri.

Navaratri Stories

Day 9

Siddhidatri

On the last day of Navaratri, we worship the form of Shakti called Siddhidatri. Siddhidatri translates to "the one who fulfills wishes."

Ma Kushmanda created the universe. She also created the first beings, including the Trimurti of Brahma, Vishnu, and Shiva. When Shiva was created, he asked the Goddess for powers or Siddhi. To do this, Kushmanda had to create another Goddess. The Goddess she created would award Shiva with 18 powers. Since this Goddess gave Siddhi, she is known as Siddhidatri.

It's also said that when Brahma was given the task of creating the world, he faced a few obstacles. Brahma needed both men and women to create. He decided to ask Ma Kushmanda for help. Siddhidatri transformed half of Shiva's body into a woman's body. This form is known as Ardhanarishvara. Brahma was able to create beings with Shiva's form.

There is a scientific reason behind the Navaratri celebration. Navaratri is attached to weather pattern changes. During this time, our immune system becomes weak, so Navaratri helps strengthen our physical and mental health.

Navaratri has an important spiritual and ritualistic significance in Hinduism. It is a rich heritage of ancient tradition.

In Hinduism, the Shakti (power and energy) is the feminine nature of the universe. Shiva, the consciousness is her consort. They both are one. Hinduism does not discriminate against male and female nature and puts them equally.

Worshiping Navaratri can be done in various ways. We learned about various Stotram, Suktam, Slokas, and Devi Pooja Sequence.

References

- Markandeya Purana
- 64 Yoginis Image: http://www.srimaakamakhya.com
- Mahakali image : TV Serial Mahakali — Anth Hi Aarambh Hai, Colors TV

Acknowledgements

- Swati Joshi (student of eYogi Gurukul) for her contribution to developing Nav Durga stories and editing this book.
- Shanvi Singh (student of eYogi Gurukul) for her contribution to developing Nav Durga stories.
- The energetic team members of eYogi Gurukul for their support and motivation: Manish Sadana, Prashant Srivastava, Dilip Kathuria, Sandeep Gupta, Satish Gupta, Vikas Vashistha, Bishember Kathuria, Ruhi Bhan, Vishal Sharma, Hemawati Nandan, Kuldeep Rawat, and Abhinav Srivastava.

Printed in Great Britain
by Amazon